1000 ideas for decorating
cupcakes, cookies & cakes

QUARRY

First published in the United States of America by
Quarry Books, a member of
Quayside Publishing Group
100 Cummings Center
Suite 406-L
Beverly, Massachusetts 01915-6101
Telephone: (978) 282-9590
Fax: (978) 283-2742
www.quarrybooks.com
Visit www.Craftside.Typepad.com for a behind-the-scenes peek at our crafty world!

Library of Congress Control Number: 2010930712

ISBN-13: 978-1-59253-651-1
ISBN-10: 1-59253-651-4

10 9 8 7 6 5 4 3 2

Design: Sandra Salamony
Front cover images (left to right, top to bottom): 223; 964; 648; 7; 635; 95; 12; 11; 2.
Back cover images (left to right): 958; 895; 16; 156.

Printed in China

1000 ideas for decorating
cupcakes, cookies & cakes

sandra salamony & gina m. brown

BEVERLY MASSACHUSETTS

QUARRY BOOKS

with frosting recipes from
Kate's Cake Decorating
by Kate Sullivan

contents

introduction

There's nothing like a dessert table, a Willy Wonka dream where everything is sweet, enticing, and edible. Even better? Seven dessert tables (some are pictured here), is what our family created when the whole town was invited to a scrumptious gala in celebration of our grandma's ninetieth birthday. We were fortunate to grow up in a family of bakers, decorators, and overall party planners, where the preparation for the event was as much fun as the party itself. But we admit that there was some resistance from us, at first.

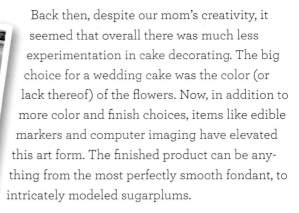

Remember grade-school bake sales? Our mother would send us to school with trays of colorful, beautifully decorated minicupcakes, which were always the first item to sell out. Once, we were foolish enough to say to Mom, "Cupcakes again? Why can't we make Rice Krispies Treats like the other families?" But, our wise mother would smile and say, "You eat with your eyes!"

Back then, despite our mom's creativity, it seemed that overall there was much less experimentation in cake decorating. The big choice for a wedding cake was the color (or lack thereof) of the flowers. Now, in addition to more color and finish choices, items like edible markers and computer imaging have elevated this art form. The finished product can be anything from the most perfectly smooth fondant, to intricately modeled sugarplums.

The following chapters present a visual feast for your inspiration: a range of confectionary treats that add magic to both special and everyday occasions. Your muse, for example, might be the seasons: the crystalline beauty of winter; the emerging flowers of spring; the sparkling celebrations of summer; or the changing displays of fall. Or, you may be attracted to the use of color, pattern, and composition. Think about how you can reinterpret a theme to create your own magic. And don't be afraid to think outside the (cake) box! An elegant entertaining cake can be a wedding cake, as can a holiday cake, as can a ... You get the idea.

Our uncle used to say, "Everything tastes better when it looks good." So, to help ensure that your creations do, in fact, look as good as possible, we have included a range of frosting recipes on page 298 to get you started, culled from *Kate's Cake Decorating,* by Kate Sullivan.

Mangia!

— *Gina M. Brown and Sandra Salamony*

elegant
entertaining

0001 – 0265

0012   Asa Hellgren, Hello Sugar!, Sweden

0013   Debbie Schwartz, Debbie's Cakes, Israel

0014   Asa Hellgren, Hello Sugar!, Sweden

0015   Asa Hellgren, Hello Sugar!, Sweden

0016   Lisa Hansen, The Whole Cake and Caboodle, New Zealand

0017 Cupcakes Nouveau, Cristina Valdes & Shayrin Badillo, USA

0018 Hana Bacova, www.flickr.com/photos/haniela, USA

0019 Layla Pegado Couto, Layla Pegado Cakes, UK

0020 Amanda Linton, House of Sweets, USA

0021   Lorena Gil V., Cupcakes & More, Switzerland

0022   Joshua Gomes, Veronica's Treats, USA

0023   The Little Cakery, (Svarna Singh), UK

0024   Elisa Brogan, www.belisacupcakes.com.au, Australia

0025   Klaire Garnica, The Little Cupcakery, Australia

0026   The Little Cakery, (Svarna Singh), UK

0027   Dimitrana Schinogl, Austria

0028   Better Bit of Butter Cookies, USA

0029   Helen Shipman, Boudoir Cakes, UK

0030   Elif Alkac Dedeoglu, Elif'in Kurabiyeleri, Turkey

0032   Rick Reichart, cakelava, USA

0033   Rick Reichart, cakelava, USA

0034   Rick Reichart, cakelava, USA

0035   Rick Reichart, cakelava, USA

0036 Rick Reichart, cakelava, USA

0037   Rick Reichart, cakelava, USA

PHOTO BY: CAKELAVA

0038   Susy Wangsawidjaja, Kuki Cupcakes, Indonesia

0039   Janet G. Bravo, The Pretty Little Cake Shop, USA

0040   Bridget Thibeault, Flour Girl, USA

PHOTO BY: SCOTT MEIVOGEL, EASY WIND STUDIO

0041   Natasha Collins, Nevie-Pie Cakes, UK

0042   Belinda Patton, www.belisacupcakes.com.au, Australia

0043	June Lynch, Picture Perfect Cake, Canada
0044	Laura-Kate Amrhein, USA
0045	Fiona Perham, sugarsugar, UK
0046	Christine Mehling, Better Bit of Butter Cookies, USA
0047	Robyn Morrison, Canada

PHOTO BY: NINA DERUBERTIS

0049   Brian & Natalie Braxton, Bratty Cakes, USA

0050   Vanessa Iti, Bella Cupcakes, New Zealand

0051   Leslie Srodek-Johnson, Stan's Northfield Bakery, USA

0052   Sylvia Rivas, Tough Cookie Bakery, USA

0053   Vanessa Iti, Bella Cupcakes, New Zealand

0054   Klaire Garnica, The Little Cupcakery, Australia

0055 Rose Petals Cakery, USA

0056 Vanessa Iti, Bella Cupcakes, New Zealand

0057 Vanessa Iti, Bella Cupcakes, New Zealand

0058 Helen Shipman, Boudoir Cakes, UK

0060	Annette Villaverde, Ladybug Luggage Gourmet Cookies & Cakes LLC, USA
0061	Toni Brancatisano, Italy
0062	Annette Villaverde, Ladybug Luggage Gourmet Cookies & Cakes LLC, USA

| 0063 | Karen Bradley, Cake Believe, USA |
| 0064 | Annette Villaverde, Ladybug Luggage Gourmet Cookies & Cakes LLC, USA |

PHOTO BY: JASON HERRING PHOTOGRAPHY

0068   Emma O'Shaughnessy, Baker's Treat, UK

0069   Colleen Davis, Little Miss Cake, USA

0070   Linda Nielsen Wermeling, Holy Sweet, Sweden

0071   Cookie Creatives by Jennifer, USA

0072   Hana Bacova, www.flickr.com/photos/haniela, USA

0073 Farnaz RouzParast Menhaji, USA

0074 Dot Klerck, Cupcakes By Design, South Africa

0075 Dina Isham, Designer Cakes by the LadyGloom, Malaysia

0076 www.fireandicing.com, USA

0077 | Lynette Horner, Cakes by Lynette, UK

0078 | Elizabeth Evenz & Erin Salerno, Elizabeth's Cakes, USA

0079   Dahlia Weinman, Dahlia's Custom Cakes, www.dahliascakes.com, USA

0080   Catie, Catie's Cakes & Cookies, Australia

0081   Rose Petals Cakery, USA

0082   Lorena Gil V., Cupcakes & More, Switzerland

0083   Christine Mehling, Better Bit of Butter Cookies, USA

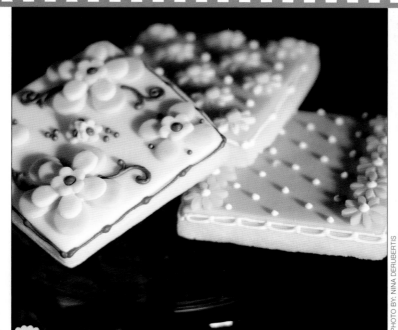

0084 Better Bit of Butter Cookies, USA

0085 The Little Cakery, (Svarna Singh), UK

0086 Dimitrana Schinogl, Austria

0087   Noemi Jaime, Mexico

0088   Emma O'Shaughnessy, Baker's Treat, UK

0089 The Cupcake Tarts,
Michelle Groenewald & Kim de Villiers, South Africa

0090 Cookie Creatives by Jennifer, USA

0091 Diane Trap, USA

0092 Janet G. Bravo, The Pretty Little Cake Shop, USA

0093	Jaime Lynne Anderson, Flutterby Cakes, UK
0094	Vanessa Iti, Bella Cupcakes, New Zealand
0095	Vanessa Iti, Bella Cupcakes, New Zealand
0096	Gumdrop Cookie Shop, USA
0097	Madeleine Farias, Madzcakes, Australia

0098   Jaime Lynne Anderson, Flutterby Cakes, UK

0099   Gabriela Cacheux, gabby cupcakes, Mexico

0100   Vanessa Iti, Bella Cupcakes, New Zealand

0102   Bridget Thibeault, Flour Girl, USA

0103   Toni Brancatisano, Italy

0104   Piamarianne, Kageriet.net, Denmark

0105   Elisa Brogan, www.belisacupcakes.com.au, Australia

0106 Shellane Pickett, Apple-Butter Bakery and Custom Cake Shoppe, USA

0107 Susana Martinez Zepeda, Casa Susana, Mexico

PHOTO BY: ALEJANDRO SERRANO FRAGOSO

0108 Shellane Pickett, Apple-Butter Bakery and Custom Cake Shoppe, USA

0109 Elisa Brogan, www.belisacupcakes.com.au, Australia

0110 Yelda Brown, Fairly Fairy Cakes, UK

0111 Dimitrana Schinogl, Austria

0112 Judy Ayre, Judy Ayre Cakes, Australia

0114   Toni Brancatisano, Italy

0115   Lynette Horner, Cakes by Lynette, UK

0116 Sumayya Eichmann, Mio Cupcakes, Australia

0117 Asa Hellgren, Hello Sugar!, Sweden

0118 Didem Resne, Turkey

0119 Lisa Hansen, The Whole Cake and Caboodle, New Zealand

0120 Taya Burke, Deliciously Decadent Cake Design, Australia

0121 Lorena Gil V., Cupcakes & More, Switzerland

| 0123 | Fiona Perham, sugarsugar, UK |

| 0124 | Jaime Lynne Anderson, Flutterby Cakes, UK |

| 0125 | Asa Hellgren, Hello Sugar!, Sweden |

| 0126 | Lisa Hansen, The Whole Cake and Caboodle, New Zealand |

| 0127 | Lorena Gil V., Cupcakes & More, Switzerland |

0128   The Little Cakery, (Svarna Singh), UK

0129   Elif Alkac Dedeoglu, Elif'in Kurabiyeleri, Turkey

0130   Lorena Gil V., Cupcakes & More, Switzerland

0131   Nancy Barinque, Canada

0132   Vanilla Bake Shop, Santa Monica, USA

0133   Gina M. Brown, USA

0134   Rose Petals Cakery, USA

PHOTO BY: JASON HERRING PHOTOGRAPHY

0135   Cupcakes Nouveau, Cristina Valdes & Shayrin Badillo, USA

0136   Kathy Finholt, USA

0137   Peggy Hambright, MagPies Bakery, USA

0138   Piamarianne, Kageriet.net, Denmark

PHOTO BY: AMANDA TAYLOR, JOHNBLACKPHOTOGRAPHY.COM

0139   Leslie Srodek-Johnson,
Stan's Northfield Bakery, USA

0140   Emma O'Shaughnessy, Baker's Treat, UK

0141   Dot Klerck, Cupcakes By Design,
South Africa

0142   Paula Ames, Cake Creations, USA

0143   Susan E. Turnbull, Anyone for Cake?, UK

0144   Fiona Perham, sugarsugar, UK

0145   Annette Villaverde, Ladybug Luggage
Gourmet Cookies & Cakes LLC, USA

0146   The Little Cakery, (Svarna Singh), UK

0147   Belinda Patton, www.belisacupcakes.com.au, Australia

0149   Sharnel Dollar, The Cupcake Company,
        Australia

0148   Dahlia Weinman, Dahlia's Custom Cakes, www.dahliascakes.com, USA

0150   Susie Hazard, SusieHazCakes, USA

0151　Lorena Gil V., Cupcakes & More, Switzerland

0152　Asa Hellgren, Hello Sugar!, Sweden

0153　Better Bit of Butter Cookies, USA

PHOTO BY: NINA DERUBERTIS

0154　Hana Bacova, www.flickr.com/photos/haniela, USA

0155 Liis Florides, www.tourtes.com, Cyprus

0156 Jen Yap, A Little Slice of Heaven, Australia

PHOTO BY: WAIKAY LAU PHOTOGRAPHY, WWW.WAIKAYLAU.COM

0157 Lisa Hansen, The Whole Cake and Caboodle, New Zealand

0158 Toni Brancatisano, Italy

0159 Layla Pegado Couto, Layla Pegado Cakes, UK

0162
June Lynch, Picture Perfect Cake, Canada

0161 Toni Brancatisano, Italy

0163 Lisa Hansen, The Whole Cake and Caboodle, New Zealand

0164   Peggy's Cupcakes, UK

0165   Cookie Creatives by Jennifer, USA

0166   The Little Cakery, (Svarna Singh), UK

0167   Belinda Patton, www.belisacupcakes.com.au, Australia

0168   Natasha Collins, Nevie-Pie Cakes, UK

0169   Debbie Coetzee, Choclit D'lites,
South Africa

0170   Valerie L. Quirarte, USA

0171   Layla Pegado Couto, Layla Pegado Cakes, UK

0172   Natasha Collins, Nevie-Pie Cakes, UK

O175   Debbie Coetzee, Choclit D'lites, South Africa

O176   Piamarianne, Kageriet.net, Denmark

O177   Monique Kleine, Cupcake Treats, Australia

O178   Monique Kleine, Cupcake Treats, Australia

O179   Debbie Coetzee, Choclit D'lites, South Africa

O180   Taya Burke, Deliciously Decadent Cake Design, Australia

0181   Marisa Hess, USA

0182   Susan Chicola, USA

0183   Dimitrana Schinogl, Austria

0184   Jennifer Bunce, The Hudson Cakery, USA

0188 Sharnel Dollar, The Cupcake Company, Australia

0189 Jen Yap, A Little Slice of Heaven, Australia

0190 Helen Shipman, Boudoir Cakes, UK

0191 www.cupcakeavenue.co.uk, UK

PHOTO BY: WAIKAY LAU PHOTOGRAPHY, WWW.WAIKAYLAU.COM

PHOTO BY: WAIKAY LAU PHOTOGRAPHY, WWW.WAIKAYLAU.COM

0192   Rene Takes the Cake, USA

0193   Jackie Rodriguez, www.lasdeliciasdevivir.com, Dominican Republic

0194   Jen Yap, A Little Slice of Heaven, Australia

0195   Sheryl Thai, Cupcake Central, Australia

0196   Linda Nielsen Wermeling, Holy Sweet, Sweden

0198 Belinda Patton, www.belisacupcakes.com.au, Australia

0199 Leah Bent, Sweet Icing Bakeshop, USA

0200 Klaire Garnica, The Little Cupcakery, Australia

0201 Leah Bent, Sweet Icing Bakeshop, USA

0202 Dot Klerck, Cupcakes By Design, South Africa

0203 Peggy Hambright, MagPies Bakery, USA

PHOTO BY: AMANDA TAYLOR, JOHNBLACKPHOTOGRAPHY.COM

0204 Dahlia Weinman, Dahlia's Custom Cakes, www.dahliascakes.com, USA

0206   Alena Vaughn, Alena's Sweets, USA

0207   Paula P. Gati, Cookie Queen LI, USA

0205   Jackie Rodriguez, www.lasdeliciasdevivir.com, Dominican Republic

0208 Belinda Patton, www.belisacupcakes.com.au, Australia

0209 Liz Shim, EatCakeBeMerry, USA

0210 Susan Chicola, USA

0211 Leisl Adams, Fancimolasses Cake Studio, Canada

0212   Bridget Thibeault, Flour Girl, USA

0213   Lisa Hansen, The Whole Cake
and Caboodle, New Zealand

0214   Annette Simpson, Canada

0215   Hana Bacova, www.flickr.com/photos/haniela, USA

Maryann Rollins, The Cookie Artisan, USA

Michelle Hollinshead, Cameo Cupcakes, UK

Robyn Morrison, Canada

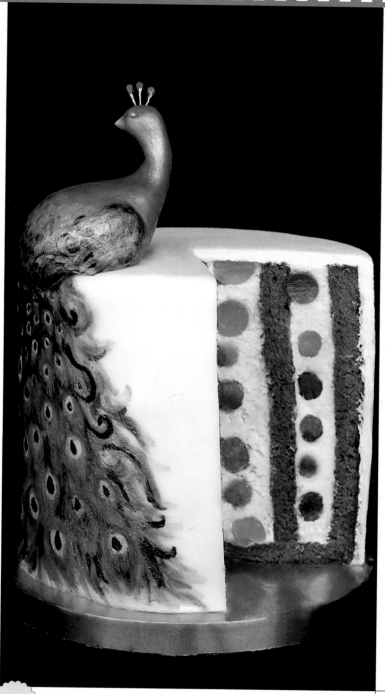

0219 Lynette Horner, Cakes by Lynette, UK

0220 Dimitrana Schinogl, Austria

0221   Annette Simpson, Canada

0222   www.roseysugar.com, Japan

0223   www.roseysugar.com, Japan

0224   Marisa Hess, USA

0226 Belinda Patton, www.belisacupcakes.com.au, Australia

0227 Debbie Schwartz, Debbie's Cakes, Israel

0228 Gumdrop Cookie Shop, USA

0229 Natasha Collins, Nevie-Pie Cakes, UK

0230 Susy Wangsawidjaja, Kuki Cupcakes, Indonesia

0231 Lisa Hansen, The Whole Cake and Caboodle, New Zealand

0232 Judy Ayre, Judy Ayre Cakes, Australia

0233 www.roseysugar.com, Japan

0234 www.belisacupcakes.com.au, Australia

0235 Brian & Natalie Braxton, Bratty Cakes, USA

0236 Lorena Gil V., Cupcakes & More, Switzerland

0237   Leah Bent, Sweet Icing Bakeshop, USA

0238   Debbie Coetzee, Choclit D'lites, South Africa

0239   Didem Resne, Turkey

0240   Debbie Schwartz, Debbie's Cakes, Israel

0241   Gabriela Cacheux, gabby cupcakes, Mexico

0242 Marie Richter, Maries Hobby Corner, Sweden

0243 Debbie Coetzee, Choclit D'lites, South Africa

0244 Taya Burke, Deliciously Decadent Cake Design, Australia

0245   Peggy's Cupcakes, UK

0246   Sylvia Rivas, Tough Cookie Bakery, USA

0247   Cristina Valdez & Shayrin Badillo, Cupcakes Nouveau, USA

0248   Amanda Rettke, USA

| 0249 | Klaire Garnica, The Little Cupcakery, Australia | 0250 | Dahlia Weinman, Dahlia's Custom Cakes, www.dahliascakes.com, USA | 0251 | Kathy Finholt, USA |

| 0252 | Klaire Garnica, The Little Cupcakery, Australia | 0253 | www.sugar-couture.com, USA |

0255   Lisa Hansen, The Whole Cake and Caboodle, New Zealand

0256   The Little Cakery, (Svarna Singh), UK

0257   Jaime Lynne Anderson, Flutterby Cakes, UK

0258   Lorena Gil V., Cupcakes & More, Switzerland

0259　Amanda Linton, House of Sweets, USA

0260　Peggy Hambright, MagPies Bakery, USA

0261　www.lookcupcake.com, USA

PHOTO BY: AMANDA TAYLOR, JOHNBLACKPHOTOGRAPHY.COM

0262　Peggy Hambright, MagPies Bakery, USA

0263　Autumn Carpenter,
Autumn Carpenter Designs, USA

0264　Marisa Hess, USA

PHOTO BY: AMANDA TAYLOR, JOHNBLACKPHOTOGRAPHY.COM

0265   Lindy Smith, www.lindyscakes.co.uk, UK

baby
& child

0266 – 0439

Colleen Davis, Little Miss Cake, USA

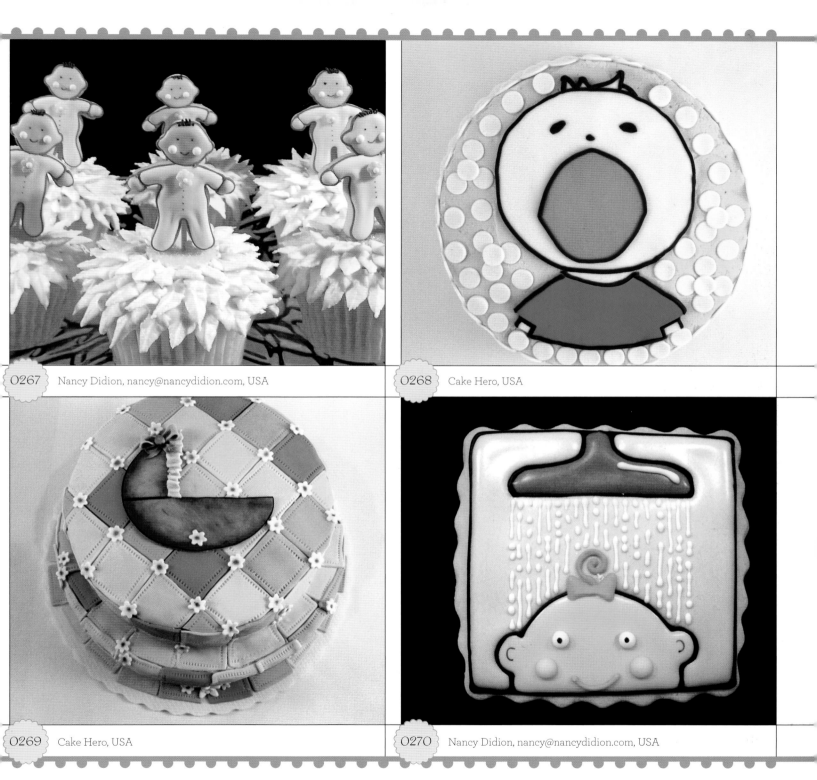

0267   Nancy Didion, nancy@nancydidion.com, USA

0268   Cake Hero, USA

0269   Cake Hero, USA

0270   Nancy Didion, nancy@nancydidion.com, USA

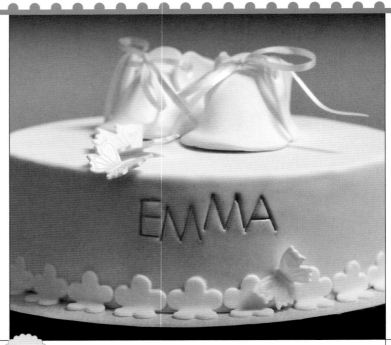

0274	Judy Ayre, Judy Ayre Cakes, Australia
0275	Scrumptious Buns, UK
0276	Hana Bacova, www.flickr.com/photos/haniela, USA
0277	Didem Resne, Turkey
0278	Sharnel Dollar, The Cupcake Company, Australia
0279	Didem Resne, Turkey
0280	Didem Resne, Turkey

0281	Marisa Hess, USA
0282	Elisa Brogan, www.belisacupcakes.com.au, Australia
0283	Susana Martinez Zepeda, Casa Susana, Mexico
0284	Yen Le, www.le-cupcake.com, Canada

0285   Jill Gosnell, Indy Cakes, USA

0286   Marie Richter, Maries Hobby Corner, Sweden

0287   Amanda Linton, House of Sweets, USA

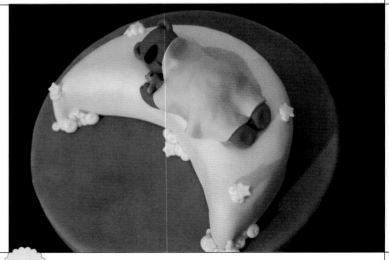

0291   Amy Stella, www.cakesuniquebyamy.com, USA

0292   Amanda Linton, House of Sweets, USA

0293   Amy Stella, www.cakesuniquebyamy.com, USA

0294   Lynette Horner, Cakes by Lynette, UK

0295   Elisa Brogan, www.belisacupcakes.com.au, Australia

0296   Colleen Davis, Little Miss Cake, USA

0297   Noemi Jaime, Mexico

0301   Gabriela Cacheux, gabby cupcakes, Mexico

0302   Dot Klerck, Cupcakes By Design, South Africa

0303   Alena Vaughn, USA

0304   Suet May Chin, Sugarcraze Arts, Malaysia

0305   www.roseysugar.com, Japan

0306 Isabel Casimiro, Pecado dos Anjos, Portugal

0307 Sylvia Rivas, Tough Cookie Bakery, USA

0308 Isabel Casimiro, Pecado dos Anjos, Portugal

0309 www.sugar-couture.com, USA

0310 Liis Florides, www.tourtes.com, Cyprus

0311 Liis Florides, www.tourtes.com, Cyprus

0312 Liis Florides, www.tourtes.com, Cyprus

0313 Liis Florides, www.tourtes.com, Cyprus

0315 Colleen Davis, Little Miss Cake, USA

0316 Colleen Davis, Little Miss Cake, USA

0318 Colleen Davis, Little Miss Cake, USA

0317 Colleen Davis, Little Miss Cake, USA

0319 Colleen Davis, Little Miss Cake, USA

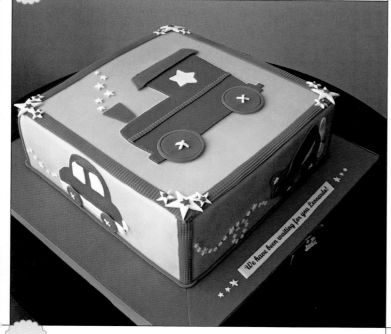

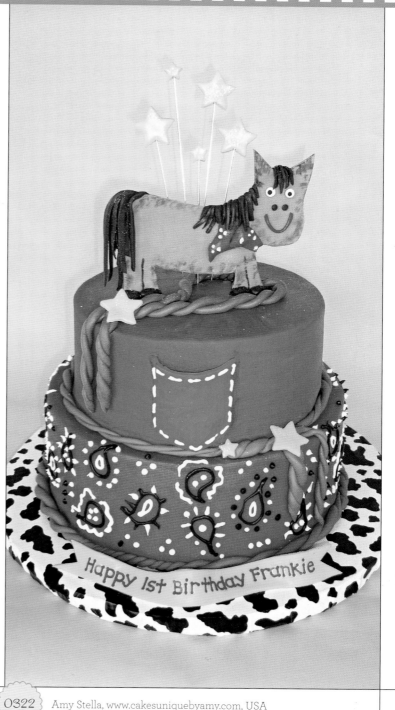

0320   Amy Stella, www.cakesuniquebyamy.com, USA

0321   Chantilly Cake Designs by Beth Aguiar, Canada

0322   Amy Stella, www.cakesuniquebyamy.com, USA

0323 Amanda Linton, House of Sweets, USA

0324 Susie Hazard, SusieHazCakes, USA

0325 Erin Salerno, USA

0326 Madeleine Farias, Madzcakes, Australia

0327   Amy Stella, www.cakesuniquebyamy.com, USA

0328   Amanda Linton, House of Sweets, USA

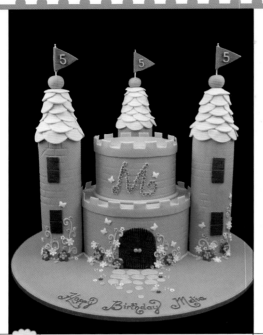

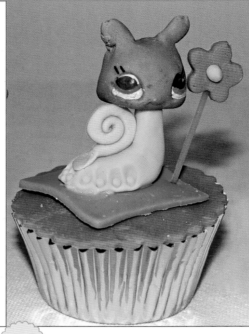

| 0329 | Michelle Rea, Inspired by Michelle Cake Designs, Australia | 0330 | Judy Ayre, Judy Ayre Cakes, Australia | 0331 | Vanessa Iti, Bella Cupcakes, New Zealand |

| 0332 | Maryann Rollins, The Cookie Artisan, USA | 0333 | Leoni Abernethy, Happy Cakes, Australia |

0335   Carla Luisa Iglesias, USA

0336   Carla Luisa Iglesias, USA

0337   Carla Luisa Iglesias, USA

0338   Carla Luisa Iglesias, USA

0339   Jen Yap, A Little Slice of Heaven, Australia

0340   Meaghan Mountford, Chic Cookies, USA

0341   Jen Yap, A Little Slice of Heaven, Australia

0342 Tammy Denmark, USA

0343 Debbie Coetzee, Choclit D'lites, South Africa

0344 Lorena Gil V., Cupcakes & More, Switzerland

0345 Michelle Rea, Inspired by Michelle Cake Designs, Australia

0346 Scrumptious Buns, UK

0347 Autumn Carpenter, Autumn Carpenter Designs, USA

0348 Amy Teoh, Mom & Daughter Cakes, Malaysia

0349 Madeleine Farias, Madzcakes, Australia

0353	Natasha Collins, Nevie-Pie Cakes, UK
0354	Lisa Hansen, The Whole Cake and Caboodle, New Zealand
0355	Toni Brancatisano, Italy

| 0356 | Marie Richter, Maries Hobby Corner, Sweden |
| 0357 | Amanda Linton, House of Sweets, USA |

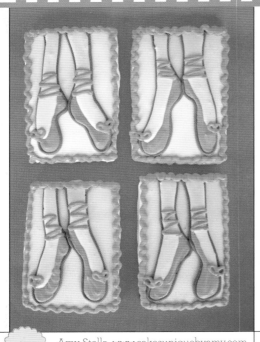

| 0358 | Amy Stella, www.cakesuniquebyamy.com, USA | 0359 | Amy Stella, www.cakesuniquebyamy.com, USA | 0360 | Adriene Brumbaugh, Shugee's, USA |

| 0361 | Elisa Brogan, www.belisacupcakes.com.au, Australia | 0362 | Susana Martinez Zepeda, Casa Susana, Mexico |

Natasha Collins, Nevie-Pie Cakes, UK

Marlyn Birmingham, Canada

Lynette Horner, Cakes by Lynette, UK

| 0366 | Judy Ayre, Judy Ayre Cakes, Australia |
| 0367 | Liis Florides, www.tourtes.com, Cyprus |

| 0368 | www.auntcakescookies.com, USA |
| 0369 | Cake Hero, USA |

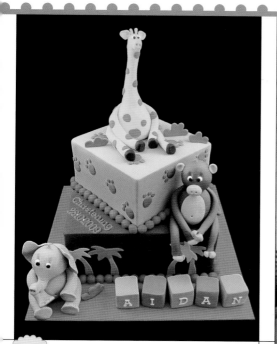

0370 Michelle Rea, Inspired by Michelle Cake Designs, Australia

0371 Jennifer Whitlock, Posh Pastries, USA

0372 Noemi Jaime, Mexico

0376	Sheryl Thai, Cupcake Central, Australia
0377	Vanessa Iti, Bella Cupcakes, New Zealand
0378	Vanessa Iti, Bella Cupcakes, New Zealand
0379	Judy Ayre, Judy Ayre Cakes, Australia

0380 Melissa Diedtrich, USA

0381 Donna Erskine, Australia

0382 Colleen Davis, Little Miss Cake, USA

0383 Colleen Davis, Little Miss Cake, USA

Nancy Didion, nancy@nancydidion.com, USA

0385   Maryann Rollins, The Cookie Artisan, USA

0386   Cassie Indari, Cakes by Cassie, Sydney, Australia

0387   Jill Gosnell, Indy Cakes, USA

0388   April Cross, USA

0389   Samantha Lee, Haus of Cake, Australia

0390   Klaire Garnica, The Little Cupcakery, Australia

0391   Emma O'Shaughnessy, Baker's Treat, UK

0392   Maryann Rollins, The Cookie Artisan, USA

0393   Suet May Chin, Sugarcraze Arts, Malaysia

0394   Lisa Hansen, The Whole Cake and Caboodle, New Zealand

0395   Nancy Didion, www.nancydidion.com, USA

0396   Madeleine Farias, Madzcakes, Australia

0397   Amy Stella, www.cakesuniquebyamy.com, USA

0398 Colleen Davis, Little Miss Cake, USA

0399 Lorena Gil V., Cupcakes & More, Switzerland

0400 Elisa Brogan, www.belisacupcakes.com.au, Australia

0401 Layla Pegado Couto, Layla Pegado Cakes, UK

0402 Renae Bradley, USA

0403 Dot Klerck, Cupcakes By Design, South Africa

0404 Tammy Denmark, USA

0405 The Little Cakery, (Svarna Singh), UK

0406 Amy Teoh, Mom & Daughter Cakes, Malaysia

0410 www.cupcakeavenue.co.uk, UK

0411 Donna Erskine, Australia

0412 Marie Richter, Maries Hobby Corner, Sweden

0413 Chantilly Cake Designs by Beth Aguiar, Canada

0414 Sumayya Eichmann, Mio Cupcakes, Australia

0415   Myriam Sánchez Garcia, chapixcookies.com, Mexico

0416   Sylvia Rivas, Tough Cookie Bakery, USA

0417   Asa Hellgren, Hello Sugar!, Sweden

0418   Anna Wawzonek, Anna Elizabeth Cakes, Canada

0419   The Cupcake Tarts, Michelle Groenewald & Kim de Villiers, South Africa

| 0420 | Brian & Natalie Braxton, Bratty Cakes, USA | 0421 | Alexandra Gardner, USA | 0422 | Colleen Davis, Little Miss Cake, USA |

| 0423 | Gabriela Cacheux, gabby cupcakes, Mexico | 0424 | Nancy Didion, nancy@nancydidion.com, USA |

baby & child   131

0425 Laura Silvana Astorino, Dulce Materia, Argentina

0426 Belinda Patton, www.belisacupcakes.com.au, Australia

0427 Gabriela Cacheux, gabby cupcakes, Mexico

0428 Autumn Carpenter, Autumn Carpenter Designs, USA

0429 Autumn Carpenter, Autumn Carpenter Designs, USA

0430   Myriam Sánchez Garcia, chapixcookies.com, Mexico

0431   Myriam Sánchez Garcia, chapixcookies.com, Mexico

0432   Myriam Sánchez Garcia, chapixcookies.com, Mexico

0433   Jen Yap, A Little Slice of Heaven, Australia

0434   Toni Brancatisano, Italy

0435   Janet G. Bravo, The Pretty Little Cake Shop, USA

0436   Donna Erskine, Australia

0437   Debbie Coetzee, Choclit D'lites, South Africa

0438   Aileen Master, A Master Creation, USA

holiday

0440 – 0581

O441   Susie Hazard, SusieHazCakes, USA

O442   www.fireandicing.com, USA

O443   Catherine Webb, www.cathysdesignercookies.com, USA

O444   Myriam Sánchez Garcia, chapixcookies.com, Mexico

PHOTO BY: MIKE WHEATLEY, CAMERA ARTS STUDIOS

0445   Meaghan Mountford, Chic Cookies, USA

0446   Meaghan Mountford, Chic Cookies, USA

0447   Meaghan Mountford, Chic Cookies, USA

0448   Meaghan Mountford, Chic Cookies, USA

0450   Piamarianne, Kageriet.net, Denmark

0451   Natasha Collins, Nevie-Pie Cakes, UK

0452   Peggy Hambright, MagPies Bakery, USA

0453   Dina Isham, Designer Cakes by the LadyGloom, Malaysia

0454   Maryann Rollins, The Cookie Artisan, USA

O455   Marisa Hess, USA

O456   Nancy Barinque, Sweet Pudgy Panda, Canada

0457   Dahlia Weinman, Dahlia's Custom Cakes, www.dahliascakes.com, USA

0458   Debbie Coetzee, Choclit D'lites, South Africa

0459   Leoni Abernethy, Happy Cakes, Australia

0460   Dimitrana Schinogl, Austria

0461   Renae Bradley, USA

0462 Dahlia Weinman, Dahlia's Custom Cakes, www.dahliascakes.com, USA

0463 Gumdrop Cookie Shop, USA

0464 The Cupcake Tarts, Michelle Groenewald & Kim de Villiers, South Africa

0465 Myriam Sánchez Garcia, www.chapixcookies.com, Mexico

0466	Loren Ebert, thebakingsheet.blogspot.com, USA
0467	Gumdrop Cookie Shop, USA
0468	Hana Bacova, www.flickr.com/photos/haniela, USA
0469	www.fireandicing.com, USA
0470	Tracy Lynn Hicks, USA

0472	Klaire Garnica, The Little Cupcakery, Australia
0473	Marieke de Korte, Alle Taarten, The Netherlands
0474	Elif Alkac Dedeoglu, Elif'in Kurabiyeleri, Turkey
0475	Patricia Holmes, Fondant.com, USA
0476	Elif Alkac Dedeoglu, Elif'in Kurabiyeleri, Turkey

0477   Amanda Rettke, USA

0478   The Little Cakery, (Svarna Singh) ,UK

0479   Shelly Netherton, Country Kitchen SweetArt, USA

0480   Meaghan Mountford, Chic Cookies, USA

0481   Jackie Rodriguez, www.lasdeliciasdevivir.com, Dominican Republic

O482 Lindy Smith, www.lindyscakes.co.uk, UK

O483 Dot Klerck, Cupcakes By Design, South Africa

O484 The Little Cakery, (Svarna Singh), UK

O485 Marlyn Birmingham, Canada

O486 Dolores Silfven and Karen Silfven, USA

O487 Marieke de Korte, Alle Taarten, The Netherlands

PHOTO BY: AMANDA TAYLOR, JOHNBLACKPHOTOGRAPHY.COM

0489 Peggy Hambright, MagPies Bakery, USA

0490 Sumayya Eichmann, Mio Cupcakes, Australia

0491 Renae Bradley, USA

0492 Amanda Rettke, USA

0493 Susie Hazard, SusieHazCakes, USA

0494   Monica Mancini, USA

0495   Brian & Natalie Braxton, Bratty Cakes, USA

0496   Patricia Holmes, Fondant.com, USA

0497   Maryann Rollins, The Cookie Artisan, USA

0498   Jeannie Gearin, cakesbyjeannie.com, USA

0499   Myriam Sánchez Garcia, chapixcookies.com, Mexico

0500   Myriam Sánchez Garcia, chapixcookies.com, Mexico

0501   Myriam Sánchez Garcia, chapixcookies.com, Mexico

0502   Myriam Sánchez Garcia, chapixcookies.com, Mexico

0507	Michelle Rea, Inspired by Michelle Cake Designs, Australia
0508	Sabrina Price, Renae Bradley, USA
0509	Sharnel Dollar, The Cupcake Company, Australia
0510	Madeleine Farias, Madzcakes, Australia
0511	Hana Bacova, www.flickr.com/photos/haniela, USA
0512	Peggy Hambright, MagPies Bakery, USA

PHOTO BY: AMANDA TAYLOR, JOHNBLACKPHOTOGRAPHY.COM

0513   Toni Brancatisano, Italy

0514   www.fireandicing.com, USA

0515   Tammy Denmark, USA

0516   www.lookcupcake.com, USA

0517   Liis Florides, www.tourtes.com, Cyprus

0518   Renae Bradley, USA

0519   Paula P. Gati, Cookie Queen LI, USA

0520 Autumn Carpenter, Autumn Carpenter Designs, USA

0521 Liis Florides, www.tourtes.com, Cyprus

0522 Cassie Indari, Cakes by Cassie, Sydney, Australia

0523 Didem Resne, Turkey

0524   Lynette Horner, Cakes by Lynette, UK

0525   Liis Florides, www.tourtes.com, Cyprus

0526   Better Bit of Butter Cookies, USA

0527   Sharnel Dollar, The Cupcake Company, Australia

0528   Valerie L. Quirarte, USA

0529   Belinda Patton,
www.belisacupcakes.com.au, Australia

0530   Scrumptious Buns, UK

0531   Amanda Linton, House of Sweets, USA

0532   Renae Bradley, USA

0533   Rose Petals Cakery, USA

0534   Debbie Coetzee, Choclit D'lites, South Africa

0535   Dahlia Weinman, Dahlia's Custom Cakes, USA

0536 Darlene Abarquez, www.make-fabulous-cakes.com, Canada

0537 Susie Hazard, SusieHazCakes, USA

0538 Catie, Catie's Cakes & Cookies, Australia

0539 Klaire Garnica, The Little Cupcakery, Australia

0540 Madeleine Farias, Madzcakes, Australia

0541   Gabriela Cacheux, gabby cupcakes, Mexico

0542   Suet May Chin, Sugarcraze Arts, Malaysia

0543   Elisa Brogan, www.belisacupcakes.com.au, Australia

0544   Marie Richter, Maries Hobby Corner, Sweden

0545 Dina Isham, Designer Cakes by the LadyGloom, Malaysia

0546 Valerie L. Quirarte, USA

0547 Susie Hazard, SusieHazCakes, USA

0548 Maryann Rollins, The Cookie Artisan, USA

0552   Michelle Hollinshead, Cameo Cupcakes, UK

0553   Didem Resne, Turkey

0554   Annette Villaverde, Ladybug Luggage
Gourmet Cookies & Cakes LLC, USA

0555   Patricia Holmes, Fondant.com, USA

0556 Didem Resne, Turkey

0557 Tracy Lynn Hicks, USA

0558 Sharon Keller, Cake it up a Notch, USA

0559 Brian & Natalie Braxton, Bratty Cakes, USA

0560　Liis Florides, www.tourtes.com, Cyprus

0561　Tammy Denmark, USA

0562　Monique Kleine, Cupcake Treats, Australia

0563　Hana Bacova, www.flickr.com/photos/haniela, USA

0564   Susie Hazard, SusieHazCakes, USA

0565   Renae Bradley, USA

0566   Samantha Potter, USA

0567   Toni Brancatisano, Italy

0568   Gumdrop Cookie Shop, USA

0569   Elif Alkac Dedeoglu, Elif'in Kurabiyeleri, Turkey

0570   Patricia Holmes, Fondant.com, USA

0571   Morgan Garrison, USA

0572   Aileen Master, A Master Creation, USA

0573   Marlyn Birmingham, Canada

0574   Maryann Rollins, The Cookie Artisan, USA

0575   Annette Villaverde, Ladybug Luggage
Gourmet Cookies & Cakes LLC, USA

0576   Brian + Natalie Braxton,
Bratty Cakes, USA

0577   www.cupcakeavenue.co.uk, UK

0578   Jaime Lynne Anderson,
Flutterby Cakes, UK

PHOTO BY: MIKE WHEATLEY, CAMERA ARTS STUDIOS

0579   Catherine Webb, www.cathysdesignercookies.com, USA

0580   Catherine Webb, www.cathysdesignercookies.com, USA

just
for fun

0582 – 0855

Alissa Levine, Pastry Girl Cakes, USA

0583   Vanessa Iti, Bella Cupcakes, New Zealand

0584   Vanessa Iti, Bella Cupcakes, New Zealand

0585   Tang Meng Choo, Mongstirs, Singapore

PHOTO BY: KENNETH WOO

0586   Shinni Tock, www.bakincow.com, Singapore

0587   Annette Villaverde, Ladybug Luggage Gourmet Cookies & Cakes LLC, USA

PHOTO BY: AMANDA TAYLOR, WWW.JOHNBLACKPHOTOGRAPHY.COM

0588   Peggy Hambright, MagPies Bakery, USA

0589   Tracy Lynn Hicks, USA

0590   Tracy Lynn Hicks, USA

0591   Tracy Lynn Hicks, USA

0592 Colleen Davis, Little Miss Cake, USA

0593 Tracy Lynn Hicks, USA

0594 Rick Reichart, cakelava, USA

0596   Meaghan Mountford, Chic Cookies, USA

0595   Nancy Didion, nancy@nancydidion.com, USA

0597   Mylene Lee, Lithia, FL, cakesbymylene@gmail.com, USA

0598　Marion Poirer, http://www.sweetopia.net, Canada

0599　Nancy Didion, nancy@nancydidion.com, USA

0600　Tracy Lynn Hicks, USA

0601　Liis Florides, www.tourtes.com, Cyprus

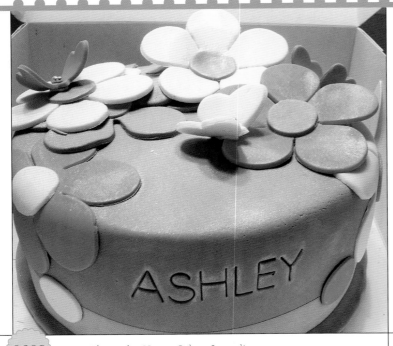

0606	Tracy Lynn Hicks, USA
0607	www.belisacupcakes.com.au, Australia
0608	www.sugar-couture.com, USA
0609	Hana Bacova, www.flickr.com/photos/haniela, USA
0610	Klaire Garnica, The Little Cupcakery, Australia

0612	Lorena Gil V., Cupcakes & More, Switzerland
0613	Didem Resne, Turkey
0614	Lisa Hansen, The Whole Cake and Caboodle, New Zealand
0615	Aileen Master, A Master Creation, USA
0616	Elisa Brogan, www.belisacupcakes.com.au, Australia

0618	Klaire Garnica, The Little Cupcakery, Australia
0619	Klaire Garnica, The Little Cupcakery, Australia
0620	Colleen Davis, Little Miss Cake, USA

0621	Marian Poirier, http://www.sweetopia.net, Canada
0622	Better Bit of Butter Cookies, USA

PHOTO BY: NINA DERUBERTIS

0623 Sylvia Rivas, Tough Cookie Bakery, USA

0624 Lynette Horner, Cakes by Lynette, UK

0625	Cyndi Coon, Laboratory5 and Sarah Spencer, Sspencer Studios, USA	0626	Samantha Potter, USA	0627	Gabriela Cacheux, gabby cupcakes, Mexico

0628	www.fireandicing.com, USA	0629	The Cupcake Tarts, Michelle Groenewald & Kim de Villiers, South Africa

0630   Lisa Hansen, The Whole Cake and Caboodle, New Zealand

0631   Maryann Rollins, The Cookie Artisan, USA

0632   Maryann Rollins, The Cookie Artisan, USA

0633   Annette Villaverde, Ladybug Luggage
Gourmet Cookies & Cakes LLC, USA

0634   Dot Klerck, Cupcakes By Design, South Africa

0635   Meaghan Mountford, Chic Cookies, USA

0636   Klaire Garnica, The Little Cupcakery, Australia

0637   www.sugar-couture.com, USA

0638   Nancy Didion, nancy@nancydidion.com, USA

0639   Natasha Collins, Nevie-Pie Cakes, UK

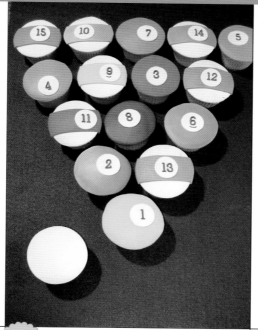

0642	www.auntcakescookies.com, USA
0643	Dana Marcus, Cupcakes By Dana, USA
0644	Leoni Abernethy, Happy Cakes, Australia

| 0645 | April Farnum, USA |
| 0646 | Tang Meng Choo, Mongstirs, Singapore |

| 0647 | Jennifer Whitlock, Posh Pastries, USA |

| 0648 | Better Bit of Butter Cookies, USA |

| 0649 | The Cupcake Tarts, Michelle Groenewald & Kim de Villiers, South Africa |

| 0650 | Piamarianne, Kageriet.net, Denmark |

0651   Dimitrana Schinogl, Austria

0652   Michelle Hollinshead,
Cameo Cupcakes, UK

0653   Natasha Collins, Nevie-Pie Cakes, UK

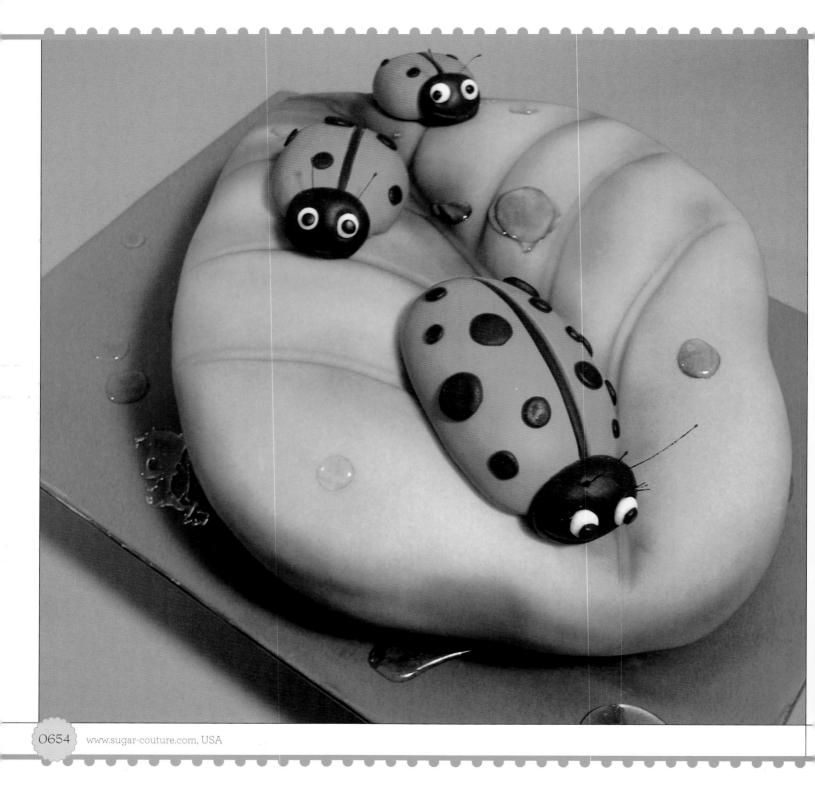

0655 Elisa Brogan, www.belisacupcakes.com.au, Australia

0656 Debbie Coetzee, Choclit D'lites, South Africa

0657 Laura-Kate Amrhein, USA

0658 Cristina Valdes & Shayrin Badillo, Cupcakes Nouveau, USA

0659   Adriene Brumbaugh, Shugee's, USA

0660   Amanda Rettke, USA

0661   Aileen Master, A Master Creation, USA

0662   Meaghan Mountford, Chic Cookies, USA

0663   Better Bit of Butter Cookies, USA

PHOTO BY NINA DERUERTIS

0664   Jennifer Whitlock, Posh Pastries, USA

0665   Isabel Casimiro, Pecado dos Anjos, Portugal

0666   Diane Trap, USA

0667   Amanda Rettke, USA

0668   Amanda Linton, House of Sweets, USA

0669   Peggy Hambright, MagPies Bakery, USA

0670   Jennifer Whitlock, Posh Pastries, USA

0671   Myriam Sánchez Garcia, chapixcookies.com, México

0672   Amy Stella, www.cakesuniquebyamy.com, USA

0673   Fiona Perham, sugarsugar, UK

0674   Fiona Perham, sugarsugar, UK

0675   Marlyn Birmingham, Canada

0676   Susy Wangsawidjaja, Kuki Cupcakes, Indonesia

| 0677 | Emily Schildhouse, USA |

| 0678 | Marisa Hess, USA |

| 0679 | Aileen Master, A Master Creation, USA |

| 0680 | Marlyn Birmingham, Canada |

| 0681 | Jill Gosnell, Indy Cakes, USA |

0682   Janet G. Bravo, The Pretty Little Cake Shop, USA

0683   Annette Villaverde, Ladybug Luggage
Gourmet Cookies & Cakes LLC, USA

0684   Better Bit of Butter Cookies, USA

0685   Amanda Rettke, USA

PHOTO BY: NINA DERUBERTIS

0686	Noemi Jaime, Mexico
0687	Klaire Garnica, The Little Cupcakery, Australia
0688	Dot Klerck, Cupcakes By Design, South Africa
0689	The Cupcake Tarts, Michelle Groenewald & Kim de Villiers, South Africa
0690	Brian & Natalie Braxton, Bratty Cakes, USA

0692   Autumn Carpenter, Autumn Carpenter Designs, USA

0693   www.fireandicing.com, USA

0694   Leoni Abernethy, Happy Cakes, Australia

0695   www.cupcakeavenue.co.uk, UK

0696   Peggy Hambright, MagPies Bakery, USA

0697   Leoni Abernethy, Happy Cakes, Australia

0698   Leoni Abernethy, Happy Cakes, Australia

0699   Leoni Abernethy, Happy Cakes, Australia

0700   Leoni Abernethy, Happy Cakes, Australia

0702   Piamarianne, Kageriet.net, Denmark

With Love

0704	Sumayya Eichmann, Mio Cupcakes, Australia
0705	Noemi Jaime, Mexico
0706	Adriene Brumbaugh, Shugee's, USA
0707	Susy Wangsawidjaja, Kuki Cupcakes, Indonesia
0708	Madeleine Farias, Madzcakes, Australia

0709	Brian & Natalie Braxton, Bratty Cakes, USA
0710	Amy Teoh, Mom & Daughter Cakes, Malaysia
0711	Jennifer Bunce, The Hudson Cakery, USA
0712	Chantilly Cake Designs by Beth Aguiar, Canada
0713	Autumn Carpenter, Autumn Carpenter Designs, USA

0714 Brian & Natalie Braxton, Bratty Cakes, USA

0715 Autumn Carpenter, Autumn Carpenter Designs, USA

0716 Maryann Rollins, The Cookie Artisan, USA

just for fun 215

O717   Debbie Schwartz, Debbie's Cakes, Israel

O718   Aileen Master, A Master Creation, USA

O719   Piamarianne, Kageriet.net, Denmark

O720   Marlyn Birmingham, Canada

O723	Asa Hellgren, Hello Sugar!, Sweden

O724	Nancy Didion, nancy@nancydidion.com, USA

O725	Maryann Rollins, The Cookie Artisan, USA

O726	Maryann Rollins, The Cookie Artisan, USA

O727	Peggy Hambright, MagPies Bakery, USA

0728   Colleen Davis, Little Miss Cake, USA

0729   Shelly Netherton, Country Kitchen SweetArt, USA

0730   Didem Resne, Turkey

0731   Jennifer Wolak, USA

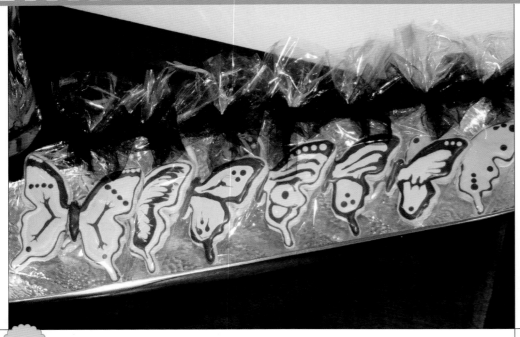

0732　Cookie Creatives by Jennifer, USA

0733　Cristina Valdes & Shayrin Badillo, Cupcakes Nouveau, USA

0734　Loren Ebert, thebakingsheet.blogspot.com, USA

0735　www.sugar-couture.com, USA

Loren Ebert, thebakingsheet.blogspot.com, USA

Madeleine Farias, Madzcakes, Australia

Rick Reichart, cakelava, USA

PHOTO BY: ABSOLUTELY LOVED/STEFANIE AND ANNA RIEDEL PHOTOGRAPHY

0739　Peggy's Cupcakes, UK

0740　Meaghan Mountford, Chic Cookies, USA

0741　Darlene Abarquez, www.make-fabulous-cakes.com, Canada

0742　Tammy Denmark, USA

0743   Jeanine Reed, Cake Muffin, USA

0744   Scrumptious Buns, UK

0745   www.sugar-couture.com, USA

0746   Lisa Hansen, The Whole Cake and Caboodle, New Zealand

0747   Donna Erskine, Australia

0748   Klaire Garnica, The Little Cupcakery, Australia

0749   Aileen Master, A Master Creation, USA

0750   Hana Bacova, www.flickr.com/photos/haniela, USA

0751	Scrumptious Buns, UK
0752	Rose Petals Cakery, USA
0753	Julaine Denny, USA
0754	Dana Marcus, Cupcakes By Dana, USA
0755	Nancy Didion, nancy@nancydidion.com, USA

RECIPE: Lemon Crème Brûlée

3 cups whipping cream
5 teaspoons grated lemon peel
¾ cup sugar
6 large egg yolks
2 teaspoons vanilla extract
¼ teaspoon salt
8 teaspoons golden brown sugar
2½-pint fresh raspberries
¼ cup Chambord or crème de cassis

0759   Colleen Davis, Little Miss Cake, USA

0760   Hana Bacova, www.flickr.com/photos/haniela, USA

0761   Catherine Webb, www.cathysdesignercookies.com, USA

0762   Jennifer Whitlock, Posh Pastries, USA

PHOTO BY: MIKE WHEATLEY, CAMERA ARTS STUDIOS

0763   http://www.sweetopia.net, Canada

0764   www.fireandicing.com, USA

0765   Susan E. Turnbull, Anyone for Cake?, UK

0766   Jennifer Wolak, USA

0767   Hana Bacova, www.flickr.com/photos/haniela, USA

0768   Dina Isham, Designer Cakes by the LadyGloom, Malaysia

0769   Sheryl Thai, Cupcake Central, Australia

0770   Valerie L. Quirarte, USA

0771   Aileen Master, A Master Creation, USA

0772   Rebecca Bendle, UK

0773   Jen Yap, A Little Slice of Heaven, Australia

0774   Asa Hellgren, Hello Sugar!, Sweden

PHOTO BY: WAIKAY LAU PHOTOGRAPHY, WWW.WAIKAYLAU.COM

0775   Tammy Denmark, USA

0776   Tracy Lynn Hicks, USA

0777   Susy Wangsawidjaja, Kuki Cupcakes, Indonesia

0778   Cookie Creatives by Jennifer, USA

0779   Shelly Netherton,
Country Kitchen SweetArt, USA

0780   www.roseysugar.com, Japan

0781   Judy Ayre, Judy Ayre Cakes, Australia

0782   Cassie Indari, Cakes by Cassie, Sydney, Australia

O783   Marlyn Birmingham, Canada

O784   Scrumptious Buns, UK

O785   Piamarianne, Kageriet.net, Denmark

0786   Shelly Netherton, Country Kitchen SweetArt, USA

0787   Liz Shim, EatCakeBeMerry, USA

0788	Peggy's Cupcakes, UK
0789	Judy Ayre, Judy Ayre Cakes, Australia
0790	Liis Florides, www.tourtes.com, Cyprus
0791	Janet G. Bravo, The Pretty Little Cake Shop, USA
0792	Hana Bacova, www.flickr.com/photos/haniela, USA

PHOTO BY: JULIE BENEDETTO, EASY WIND STUDIO

0793 Bridget Thibeault, Flour Girl, USA

0794 Meaghan Mountford, Chic Cookies, USA

0795 Meaghan Mountford, Chic Cookies, USA

0796 Ninotchka Beavers, USA

0797   Michelle Rea, Inspired by Michelle Cake Designs, Australia

0798   Madeleine Farias, Madzcakes, Australia

0799   Marian Poirier, http://www.sweetopia.net, Canada

0800   Lisa Hansen, The Whole Cake and Caboodle, New Zealand

0801   Rose Petals Cakery, USA

0802   Laura-Kate Amrhein, USA

0803	Lisa Hansen, The Whole Cake and Caboodle, New Zealand
0804	Susana Martinez Zepeda, Casa Susana, Mexico
0805	Alissa Levine, Pastry Girl Cakes, USA

| 0806 | Catie, Catie's Cakes & Cookies, Australia |
| 0807 | Susie Hazard, SusieHazCakes, USA |

0808   Brian & Natalie Braxton,
Bratty Cakes, USA

0809   Dahlia Weinman, Dahlia's Custom Cakes,
www.dahliascakes.com, USA

0810   Vanessa Iti, Bella Cupcakes,
New Zealand

0811   Nancy Didion, nancy@nancydidion.com, USA

0812   Nancy Didion, nancy@nancydidion.com, USA

| 0813 | Chantilly Cake Designs by Beth Aguiar, Canada |

| 0814 | The Cupcake Tarts, Michelle Groenewald & Kim de Villiers, South Africa |

| 0815 | Renae Bradley, USA |

| 0816 | Dina Isham, Designer Cakes by the LadyGloom, Malaysia |

0817 Amy Stella, www.cakesuniquebyamy.com, USA

0818 Layla Pegado Couto, Layla Pegado Cakes, UK

0819 Catie, Catie's Cakes & Cookies, Australia

0820 Marlyn Birmingham, Canada

0821	Nancy Didion, nancy@nancydidion.com, USA
0822	April Farnum, USA
0823	Judy Ayre, Judy Ayre Cakes, Australia
0824	Dina Isham, Designer Cakes by the LadyGloom, Malaysia
0825	Susy Wangsawidjaja, Kuki Cupcakes, Indonesia

0826	Melissa Diedtrich, USA
0827	Amy Teoh, Mom & Daughter Cakes, Malaysia
0828	Brian & Natalie Braxton, Bratty Cakes, USA
0829	Colleen Davis, Little Miss Cake, USA
0830	Renae Bradley, USA

0831 Bridget Thibeault, Flour Girl, USA

0832 Belinda Patton, www.belisacupcakes.com.au, Australia

0833 Sumayya Eichmann, Mio Cupcakes, Australia

0834 Amy Stella, www.cakesuniquebyamy.com, USA

0839 Leoni Abernethy, Happy Cakes, Australia

0840 Scrumptious Buns, UK

0841 Amy Teoh, Mom & Daughter Cakes, Malaysia

0842 Colleen Davis, Little Miss Cake, USA

0843   www.auntcakescookies.com, USA

0844   Debbie Coetzee,
Choclit D'lites, South Africa

0845   Monica Williams, Delissimon,
New Zealand

0846   Monica Williams, Delissimon, New Zealand

0847   Christine Mehling, Better Bit of Butter Cookies, USA

PHOTO BY: NINA DERUBERTIS

0848   Erin Salerno, USA

0849   Marian Poirier, http://www.sweetopia.net, Canada

0850   Melissa Diedtrich, USA

0851 Nayeli Hartman,
Itty Bitty Cake Shop, USA

0852 Sheryl Thai, Cupcake Central, Australia

0853 Leoni Abernethy, Happy Cakes, Australia

0854 Adriene Brumbaugh, Shugee's, USA

weddings
& engagements
0856 – 1000

0857   www.sugar-couture.com, USA

0858   The Little Cakery, (Svarna Singh), UK

0859   Linda Nielsen Wermeling, Holy Sweet, Sweden

0860   Chantilly Cake Designs by Beth Aguiar, Canada

0862 Kathy Finholt, Kathy's Kakes, LLC, USA

0861 Lindy Smith, www.lindyscakes.co.uk, UK

0863 Judy Ayre, Judy Ayre Cakes, Australia

0864   Liz Shim, EatCakeBeMerry, USA

0865   Rick Reichart, cakelava, USA

0866   Marieke de Korte, Alle Taarten, The Netherlands

PHOTO BY: DAVEMIYAMOTO.COM

0867   Vanessa Iti, Bella Cupcakes, New Zealand

0868   Kathy Finholt, USA

0871 Cecille L. Sia, Tongued-Tied With Sweetest Delight Cakes & Pastry, Philippines

0872 Jen Yap, A Little Slice of Heaven, Australia

0873 Taya Burke, Deliciously Decadent Cake Design, Australia

0874 Linda Nielsen Wermeling, Holy Sweet, Sweden

0875 Jen Yap, A Little Slice of Heaven, Australia

0876 Rick Reichart, cakelava, USA

0877 Michelle Rea, Inspired by Michelle Cake Designs, Australia

0878   Sylvia Rivas, Tough Cookie Bakery, USA

0879   Marisa Hess, USA

0880   Sharnel Dollar,
The Cupcake Company, Australia

0881   Piamarianne, Kageriet.net, Denmark

0882   Sharon Keller, Cake it up a Notch, USA

0883   Taya Burke, Deliciously Decadent Cake Design, Australia

0884   Taya Burke, Deliciously Decadent Cake Design, Australia

0885   Marisa Hess, USA

0886   Belinda Patton, www.belisacupcakes.com.au, Australia

0887   Elif Alkac Dedeoglu, Elif'in Kurabiyeleri, Turkey

0888   Jene Nato a/k/a Rylan Ty, USA

0889   Taya Burke, Deliciously Decadent Cake Design, Australia

0891 Vanessa Iti, Bella Cupcakes, New Zealand

0892 Jen Yap, A Little Slice of Heaven, Australia

0893 Belinda Patton, www.belisacupcakes.com.au, Australia

0894 Chantilly Cake Designs by Beth Aguiar, Canada

0896   Liis Florides, www.tourtes.com, Cyprus

0895   Toni Brancatisano, Italy

0897   Laura-Kate Amrhein, USA

0898　Sharon Keller, Cake it up a Notch, USA

0899　Janice Boyd, USA

0900　Elizabeth Evenz & Erin Salerno, Elizabeth's Cakes, USA

0901 Peggy Hambright, MagPies Bakery, USA

0902 Piamarianne, Kageriet.net, Denmark

0903 Jennifer Bunce,
The Hudson Cakery, USA

0904 Taya Burke, Deliciously Decadent
Cake Design, Australia

0905 Peggy's Cupcakes, UK

0906 Linda Nielsen Wermeling, Holy Sweet,
Sweden

0907 Toni Brancatisano, Italy

0908   Chantilly Cake Designs by Beth Aguiar, Canada

0909   Chantilly Cake Designs by Beth Aguiar, Canada

0910   Chantilly Cake Designs by Beth Aguiar, Canada

0911   Chantilly Cake Designs by Beth Aguiar, Canada

0913   Liz Shim, EatCakeBeMerry, USA

0914	Cookie Creatives by Jennifer, USA
0915	Kathy Finholt,, USA
0916	Cookie Creatives by Jennifer, USA
0917	Cookie Creatives by Jennifer, USA
0918	Lindy Smith, www.lindyscakes.co.uk, UK

0919 Debbie Schwartz, Debbie's Cakes, Israel

0920 Alison Sturge,
      Alison Wonderland Cakes, USA

0921 Farnaz RouzParast Menhaji, USA

0922 Marisa Hess, USA

0923 Nancy Didion, nancy@nancydidion.com, USA

0925   Kathy Finholt, Kathy's Kakes, LLC, USA

0926   Kathy Finholt, Kathy's Kakes, LLC, USA

0927   Chantilly Cake Designs by Beth Aguiar, Canada

0928   Vanilla Bake Shop, Santa Monica, USA

0929   Paula Ames, Cake Creations, USA

0930   Lindy Smith, www.lindyscakes.co.uk, UK

PHOTO BY: JASON HERRING PHOTOGRAPHY

0931 Lydia C. Carter, Celene's Cuisine, USA

0932 Amy Stella,
www.cakesuniquebyamy.com, USA

0933 Alena Vaughn, USA

0935   Susie Hazard, SusieHazCakes, USA

0934   Rick Reichart, cakelava, USA

0936   Cookie Creatives by Jennifer, USA

0937 Gabriela Cacheux, gabby cupcakes, Mexico

0938 Adriene Brumbaugh, Shugee's, USA

0939 Emma O'Shaughnessy, Baker's Treat, UK

0940 Gabriela Cacheux, gabby cupcakes, Mexico

0941 Rick Reichart, cakelava, USA

0942 Jen Yap, A Little Slice of Heaven, Australia

0943 Cindy J. Patrick, Enticing Icings and Custom Cakes, USA

0950   Lindy Smith, www.lindyscakes.co.uk, UK

0951   Jennifer Bunce,
The Hudson Cakery, USA

0952   Helen Shipman, Boudoir Cakes, UK

0953 Didem Resne, Turkey

0954 Alena Vaughn, USA

0955 Liis Florides, www.tourtes.com, Cyprus

0956 Chantilly Cake Designs by Beth Aguiar, Canada

0957 Peggy Hambright, MagPies Bakery, USA

0958 Rick Reichart, cakelava, USA

0959   Dahlia Weinman, Dahlia's Custom Cakes, www.dahliascakes.com, USA

0960   June Lynch, Picture Perfect Cake, Canada

0961   Darlene Abarquez, www.make-fabulous-cakes.com, Canada

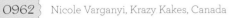

0962   Nicole Varganyi, Krazy Kakes, Canada

0963   Marisa Hess, USA

0965   Patricia Holmes, Fondant.com, USA

0964   Liz Shim, EatCakeBeMerry, USA

0966   Linda Nielsen Wermeling, Holy Sweet, Sweden

| 0967 | Gina Milton, Just Desserts, USA |

| 0968 | Yuhalini Narendran, Party With Cakes, Malaysia |

| 0969 | Helen Shipman, Boudoir Cakes, UK |

| 0970 | June Lynch, Picture Perfect Cake, Canada |

| 0971 | Gumdrop Cookie Shop, USA |

| 0972 | Marisa Hess, USA |

PHOTO BY: VALERIA SAVOY, KILLER IMAGE

0973 Marisa Hess, USA

0974 Anna Wawzonek, Anna Elizabeth Cakes, Canada

0975 Taya Burke, Deliciously Decadent Cake Design, Australia

0976 Marlyn Birmingham, Canada

0977 Scrumptious Buns, UK

0978   Bridget Thibeault, Flour Girl, USA

0979   Marisa Hess, USA

0980   Erin Salerno, USA

0981   Cecille L. Sia, Tongue-Tied With Sweetest Delight Cakes & Pastry, Philippines

0982   Alena Vaughn, USA

0983   Alena Vaughn, USA

0984   Lindy Smith, www.lindyscakes.co.uk, UK

0985   Bridget Thibeault, Flour Girl, USA

0986   Liz Shim, EatCakeBeMerry, USA

| 0987 | Amy Stella, www.cakesuniquebyamy.com, USA | 0988 | Peggy's Cupcakes, UK | 0989 | Sylvia Rivas, Tough Cookie Bakery, USA |

| 0990 | Anna Wawzonek, Anna Elizabeth Cakes, Canada | 0991 | Rose Petals Cakery, USA |

0992   Didem Resne, Turkey

0993   Samantha Lee, Haus of Cake, Australia

0994   June Lynch, Picture Perfect Cake, Canada

0995 Dahlia Weinman, Dahlia's Custom Cakes, www.dahliascakes.com, USA

0996 Michelle Rea, Inspired by Michelle Cake Designs, Australia

0997 Brian & Natalie Braxton, Bratty Cakes, USA

0998 Robyn Morrison, Canada

0999 Hana Bacova, www.flickr.com/photos/haniela, USA

frosting recipes

excerpted from *Kate's Cake Decorating* by Kate Sullivan

meringue buttercream

Fluffy, silky-smooth meringue buttercream icing provides both a substantial cake filling and a just-right, creamy consistency for decorating.

MAKES 4 CUPS

> 2 cups (4 sticks; 450 g) unsalted butter, room temperature
> 1 tablespoon (15 ml) pure vanilla extract
> 5 large egg whites
> 1 ¼ cups (250 g) granulated sugar

1. In a mixing bowl, cream the butter. Blend in the vanilla. Set aside.

2. In the bowl of an electric mixer, combine the egg whites and sugar. Set the bowl over a pan of simmering water and whisk continuously until the sugar has dissolved, 3 to 5 minutes.

3. Mix on high speed using the whisk attachment, until firm, glossy peaks form, about 4 minutes.

4. Reduce the speed to low, and add the creamed butter, about a cup at a time, to the meringue. Beat until smooth.

Don't worry if the buttercream seems to break down and curdle when the butter is added to the eggs. Just continue to beat it until it smoothes back out to a soft, creamy texture.

Use immediately or refrigerate in an airtight container for up to one week. To restore consistency, bring back to room temperature and stir with a stiff rubber spatula or electric mixer.

VARIATION
For chocolate meringue buttercream, add 1 part ganache (page 299) to 4 parts meringue buttercream recipe.

simple buttercream

This is a good shortcut recipe, sweet and simple. The trade off: It's not quite as smooth or subtle as the meringue buttercream, but many people prefer using it for decorations that call for buttercream because it's more stable.

MAKES 5 CUPS

> 1 cup (2 sticks; 225 g) unsalted butter, room temperature
> 4 cups (910 g) confectioners' sugar
> ½ cup (120 ml) milk
> 2 teaspoons (10 ml) vanilla extract (or other flavor)
> ⅛ teaspoon salt

1. Combine all ingredients in a large mixing bowl fitted with a paddle attachment. Beat on medium speed until smooth, about 2 to 3 minutes, occasionally scraping down the sides of the bowl.

Use immediately or refrigerate in an airtight container for up to two weeks. To restore consistency, bring back to room temperature and stir with a stiff rubber spatula or electric mixer.

VARIATION
For chocolate buttercream, add 6 ounces (170 g) semisweet chocolate (melted and cooled) to simple buttercream recipe.

an easy, foolproof ganache

Ganache isn't just a chocolate lover's dream, even though it's a giant chocolate truffle of a filling—it's a cake maker's delight. It makes a wonderful sturdy base coat for a cake that will later be covered in fondant. It's the one thing I can't resist sampling while making a cake. Adding Cointreau gives it a nice orangey flavor and warmth.

MAKES 3 CUPS

> 18 ounces (510 g) semisweet chocolate chips
> (or block semisweet chocolate, finely chopped)
> 1 ½ cups (355 ml) heavy cream
> 1 tablespoon (15 ml) liqueur or flavor (optional)

1. Place the chocolate pieces in a large heatproof bowl.

2. Bring cream just about to a boil over medium-high heat. Pour over chopped chocolate.

3. Cover and let stand 10 minutes.

4. Whisk the chocolate and cream (and add flavor if desired) until well combined; dark, smooth, and glossy.

5. Let sit at room temperature until cooled. To thicken, beat with hand mixer for a few minutes. It also thickens over time as it sits.

Refrigerate in an airtight container for up to a week. To restore to spreading or glazing consistency, heat and stir over double boiler for a few minutes until softened.

perfect royal icing

This smooth, white, hard-drying icing holds its shape when you're piping decorations. It's also used as a glue to connect decorations. It's sensitive to heat and humidity, and also to grease, so keep it cool and make sure your utensils have been cleansed thoroughly of butter and oil.

MAKES ABOUT 2 CUPS

> 2 large egg whites, room temperature
> 4 cups (910 g) confectioners' sugar
> Juice of ½ lemon

1. Beat the egg whites on medium speed to loosen, about a minute.

2. Add sugar about a cup at a time, beating continuously until stiff but not dry, about 4 to 5 minutes. Add lemon juice.

Refrigerate in an airtight container for up to a week. To restore to piping consistency, stir with a stiff rubber spatula.

tips

*If icing is too thick, add more egg white;
if it is too thin, add more sugar.*

Don't use raw eggs in icing made for pregnant women, young children, or people with immune deficiencies. Meringue powder, which is available at cake-supply shops, is a safe alternative; the packaging will carry a recipe for royal icing.

To make a thinner royal icing for flooding borders, gradually add a little water at a time until the icing has a syrupy consistency.

fondant

Fondant is a pliable, doughlike icing that's rolled out with a rolling pin. It's then draped over a cake and coaxed to fit like a glove. Even with fondant-covered cakes prominently featured in wedding magazines over the past several years, the porcelain-smooth finish of rolled fondant still turns a lot of heads in appreciation and wonder. It will keep a cake fresh for several days. Fondant can also be sculpted into decorations.

**MAKES ENOUGH TO COVER A 9-INCH (23 CM) CAKE,
4 INCHES (10 CM) HIGH**

RECIPE 1:

Buy ready-made! It tastes just as good and it's about 10,000 times less work.

pounds of fondant per tier size

TIER SIZE (3 inches [9 cm] high)	POUNDS (KG) OF FONDANT Round, octagonal, petal, or hexagonal tiers	POUNDS (KG) OF FONDANT Square tiers
6-inch (15 cm) cake	1 (0.7 kg)	2 (0.9 kg)
8-inch (20 cm) cake	2 (0.9 kg)	2 (1 kg)
10-inch (25 cm) cake	2 (1 kg)	3 (1.3 kg)
12-inch (30 cm) cake	3 (1.3 kg)	4 (1.8 kg)
14-inch (35 cm) cake	4 (1.8 kg)	5 (2.2 kg)
16-inch (40 cm) cake	5 (2.2 kg)	6 (3 kg)
18-inch (45 cm) cake	6 (3 kg)	—

This table allows for extra fondant to be trimmed from each tier: It's always best to have too much rather than too little. The excess can be wrapped tightly and reused.

RECIPE 2:

1 tablespoon (14 g) unflavored gelatin
¼ cup (60 ml) cold water
½ cup (150 g) glucose or white corn syrup
1 tablespoon (14 g) glycerin
1 teaspoon (5 ml) flavoring (pure vanilla extract will impart a hint of ivory color; clear extracts are best if you want a pure white fondant)
4 cups (910 g) sifted confectioners' sugar

1. Combine gelatin and cold water in top of double boiler and let stand until softened (about 5 minutes). Heat until dissolved and clear.

2. Remove from heat and add the glucose (or syrup), glycerin, and flavoring. Mix well.

3. Place 3 cups (700 g) confectioners' sugar in a bowl and make a well. Slowly pour the gelatin mixture into the well and mix until sugar is blended.

4. Use a rubber spatula to scrape down sides of bowl and remove the sticky fondant to a clean work surface. Knead in remaining cup (210 g) of confectioners' sugar, a little at a time until the fondant is smooth, pliable, and doesn't stick to your hands.

5. Roll the fondant into a smooth ball and wrap in plastic. Place in an airtight container in a cool, dry place to set overnight.

If fondant is too soft, add more sugar; if too stiff, add water (a scant drop at a time).

Fondant can be kept for several months sealed tightly in a plastic bag inside an airtight container. Do not refrigerate or freeze. When ready to use, knead again until soft.

gumpaste

Gumpaste is a pliable, doughlike mixture that can be rolled very thin to make lifelike flowers or bows and can be shaped into berries or banners and all sorts of things. Technically it's edible, but don't expect much: it's bland and cardboardlike. The consistency should be pliable but not sticky; it should snap when pulled apart. It works best when it's aged for a few days.

> 1 cup (125 g) gumpaste mix (available at cake
>   suppliers)
> 1 tablespoon (14 ml) hot water
> Vegetable shortening, for greasing

1. Combine 1 cup (125 g) of the mix with the water in a small, lightly greased glass or ceramic mixing bowl.

2. When completely blended, gradually work in the balance of the mix by kneading into a ball. Grease the surface of the ball lightly with vegetable shortening and wrap well in plastic.

3. Place in an airtight container in a cool, dry place to set for 12 to 24 hours before using.

If the paste is too sticky, add a little bit of the powdered mix; if too stiff, add a touch of shortening.

Since the ingredients for making gumpaste from scratch are specific to specialty cake-supply stores, and there's no taste advantage for homemade over the mix, the gumpaste mix is a very good way to go.

Gumpaste can be kept for several months sealed tightly in a plastic bag inside an airtight container.

marzipan

Made from icing sugar, almonds, and eggs, marzipan has been around for centuries, and it's used all over the world. It's like a fragrant sweet clay from which you can fashion all sorts of figures, fruits, and other decorations. I prefer it to other modeling pastes for its taste and appealingly dense texture. And, I have to admit, I always use ready-made marzipan. It works and tastes great, and it can be found in most grocery stores.

MAKES 2 POUNDS (0.9 KG)

> 1 pound (455 g) almond paste, cut into pieces
> 2 cups (455 g) confectioners' sugar
> ¼ cup (75 g) light corn syrup or glucose
> Vegetable shortening, for hands

1. Combine almond paste, the confectioners' sugar, and corn syrup in a large mixing bowl. Knead the mixture with your hands (first rub hands with a light coating of vegetable shortening to prevent sticking).

2. Shape into a ball and wrap well in plastic wrap; place in an airtight container until ready for use.

Refrigerate in an airtight container for up to four months.

image directory

0001 Chocolate Cloud: chocolate ganache glaze, hand-spun sugar

0002 Love Heart Cupcake: piped dark chocolate

0003 Sunny Cupcake: walnut cupcake, fondant icing, handmade fondant flowers, brushed with luster dust

0004 Gingerbread Cupcakes: lemon frosting

0005 Super Spicy Gingerbread Cupcakes with Fresh Lemon Glaze: egg-free gingerbread cupcakes glazed with fresh lemon-butter glaze

0006 Petal Flower Cupcakes: piped buttercream

0007 Happy Daisy Cupcakes: piped buttercream

0008 Cherry Blossom Cupcakes: piped buttercream

0009 Hydrangea Cupcakes: piped buttercream

0010 Three-Tier Mini Birthday Cake: fondant

0011 Garden Party: piped buttercream on cupcakes, fondant-covered cake, fondant decorations

0012 Coconut Strawberry Cupcakes: fondant decorations

0013 Pink Joy: rolled fondant

0014 Rhubarb Raspberry Cupcakes: fondant brushed with luster dust

0015 Cupcake Tea Party: fondant decorations

0016 Paisley-Inspired Cookies: rolled fondant, piped royal icing, painted gel coloring

0017 Red Rose Cupcake: fresh, red tea rose on meringue frosting with satin ribbon

0018 Red Poppy: lemon ricotta cupcake, handmade fondant red poppy

0019 Brigadeiro Cake: chocolate ganache, chopped chocolate, chocolate transfer sheet

0020 Black Forest Cupcakes: piped whipped cream, topped with cherry

0021 Red Garden: poured fondant, handmade gumpaste flower

0022 Chocolate Cake Pops: dipped, decorated

0023 Summer Fruits Basket: chocolate scrolls, buttercream

0024 Red Poppy: red gumpaste flower using daisy cutter, black sparkle

0025 Red Daisies: piped dark chocolate, rolled fondant

0026 The Henna Collection: hand painting on sugarpaste

0027 Tea Cookies: colored cookie dough

0028 Various Daisies: rolled fondant, royal icing

0029 Cupcakes: orange buttercream, sugar flowers

0030 Orange Flower Cookies: rolled fondant, embossed, molded flowers

0031 Birdcage Cake: piped royal icing, rolled fondant

0032 B & B Cake: striped fondant with handcrafted floral vine

0033 Anamarie: chocolate wrapped with piped floral vine

0034 Bonnie: fondant with handcrafted phalaenopsis orchids

0035 Sunset Bamboo: fondant with color gradation, hibiscus appliqué & handcrafted bamboo

0036 Pillows Cake: sculpted fondant stacked Indian pillows & handcrafted jewel accents

0037 Bird of Paradise: fondant hand painted with bird of paradise appliqué

0038 Orange Cuppies: buttercream swirl, mandarin orange

0039 Fall Flower Cupcakes: chocolate buttercream icing, fondant decorations

0040 Spring Sprinkle Cupcakes: vanilla buttercream

0041 Tropical Cupakes: buttercream swirl with hand-painted fondant disk

0042 Tropical Blooms: embossed fondant circle cutout topped with blooms, buttercream

0043 Green Orchids: rolled fondant, gumpaste green cymbidium orchids

0044 Pink Floral Mini Cakes: petit four techniques, fondant cutouts

0045 Flower Celebration Cake: candy-striped detail, handmade sugar flowers

0046 Summer Garden: rolled fondant, royal icing

0047 Gerbera Daisies Cake: fondant, gumpaste daisies

0048 Spring Cupcakes: fondant, handmade toppers

0049 Purple Rose Cupcakes: five-petal rose cutter, dragees

0050 Hot Pink & Black: fondant

0051 Brandi Cake: satin ice fondant, fondant cutouts, edible glitter, gumpaste lilies, piped buttercream writing

0052 Black & White Striped Cake: fondant, gumpaste embellishments

0053 Hot Red: fondant, embossing

0054 Purple Blossoms: rolled fondant, flower cutter

0055 Heart Sugar Cookies: stenciled royal icing

0056 Whimsical & Fairylike: fondant, sugar pearls, embossing

0057 Leftovers: buttercream, fondant

0058 Special Occasion Cake: chocolate cigarillos, fresh roses

0059 Blue & Green Modern Floral: chocolate transfer sheet, chocolate piping

0060 Panda Bear: hand-painted, colored rolled fondant

0061 Snowflake Cookies: sugar cookies, fondant, luster dust

0062 Butterfly Cupcake: hand-painted, rolled fondant

0063 Blue & White Scrollwork: piped buttercream, hand-drawn chocolate monogram

0064 Double Fish: hand-painted, colored rolled fondant

0065 Double-Tier Birthday Cake: rolled fondant, sugar flowers, diamante detail

0066 Stenciled Fern Cookies: sugar cookie, royal icing

0067 Black & White Cameo Cake: hand-rolled, black fondant, piped Swiss dot borders, sugar cameo accents

0068 After Eight Cupcakes: piped buttercream, flower paste decoration, dragee

0069 Grasshopper Cupcakes: piped buttercream icing & fresh mint leaf

0070 O'Apple Blossom: buttercream, sugar, & fabric blossom

0071 Winter Trees Cookie: sugar cookie, royal icing

0072 Flower Cupcake: cream cheese vanilla frosting, fondant flower, luster dust

0073 Cupcakes Display: sugar & fondant decoration

0074 Shades of Orange: embossed fondant, handmade fondant roses

0075 Patterned Mini Cakes: rolled fondant, piped royal icing

0076 Maple Leaves: piped royal icing, flooding, marbling

0077 Winter Jewel Cupcakes: fondant

0078 Mosaic Dummy Cake: rolled fondant, hand-cut fondant tiles

0079 Crowning Glory: fondant, gumpaste, airbrushing

0080 Coconut Rough Cupcakes: homemade truffles, coconut cupcake

0081 Fall Leaf Cupcakes: candy clay in leaf mold

0082 Chocolate Dream: piped white chocolate, handmade plastic chocolate flowers

0083 Fall Mini Bouquets: rolled fondant, royal icing

0084 Climbing Clematis, Daisy Garden, Spring Daisy: rolled fondant, royal icing detail

0085 Spring Petunia Blossom: buttercream swirl, sugarpaste flower made with veining mold

0086 Nougat Cake: almond marzipan, rolled fondant, nougat filling

0087 Caramelo: Italian frosting, strawberries, caramel

0088 Jane: rolled fondant, flower paste, fondant cutouts, dragee centers

0089 Gorgeous Gerbera: silicone molded fondant

0090 Claret Snowflake Cookies: sugar cookie, royal icing

0091 Strawberry Clowns: chocolate dip, piped ruffle, strawberry

0092 Bi-Color Cupcake Swirl: buttercream in two colors

0093 Cookie Favors: sugar cookies with personalized fondant

0094 Small Parcel of Sweetness: fondant, buttercream

0095 Shabby Chic: fondant, buttercream

0096 Blossom Cookie: original design on edible sugar paper

0097 Sprinkles & Flowers Cupcakes: rolled fondant

0098 Blue & Brown Cupcakes: aqua-colored lemon poured fondant topping adorned with chocolate decoration with gold accents

0099 Shabby Chic Roses: fondant, sugar flowers, piped royal icing

0100 Let's Celebrate: fondant, buttercream

0101 Daisies Cake: fondant embellishments, chocolate

0102 Polka Dot Party Cake: chocolate fondant, royal icing

0103 Petit Four with Tea Cup: embossed fondant, gros-grain ribbon

0104 Pretzel Bites: milk chocolate pretzels, paradise nuts

0105 Antique Blossom: dogwood rose cutter/veiner in ivory gumpaste, hearts overflowing laser wrapper

0106 Red Floral Scrolls: rolled fondant, hand-painted silver, impression mat

0107 Doily: rolled fondant, cutout, piped royal icing

0108 Mini Bouquet of Roses: rolled fondant

0109 Daisy Swirl: white swirl embossed fondant disk, yellow & orange daisy using calyx cutter, pearl luster spray

0110 Rose Cupcakes: fondant, hand-molded sugar flowers

0111 Roses Cake: rolled & hand-formed fondant, embellishments

0112 Frangipani Topper: gumpaste flowers

0113 Mini Blossom Cake: chocolate mini cake, rolled fondant, fondant flowers & butterflies

0114 Two-Tier Feminine Cake: fondant, luster dust, gumpaste butterflies, decorative brooch

0115 Retro Floral Wedding Cake: fondant

0116 Winter Wonderland: rolled fondant shapes

0117 Vanilla Cupcakes: piped buttercream, fondant decorations

0118 Birthday Flower Cookie: fondant

0119 Almond & Chocolate: rolled & embossed fondant, piped royal icing, brushed luster dusts

0120 The Aquatic Wrap: rolled fondant, gumpaste flowers

0121 Ti Voglio Bene: air-brushed rolled fondant, handmade sugar flowers

0122 Dragonfly Cup & Cupcake: fondant cup & saucer, handmade fondant flowers & dragonfly, embossed, ruffled edges

0123 Chocolate Celebration Cake: chocolate fondant, embossed lettering, gold luster detail

0124 Blossom Cake: frilly flowers & piped royal icing design

0125 Blueberry-Filled Lemon Cupcake: fondant brushed with luster dust

0126 Rose Wedding Cupcake/Single Cake: chocolate molded bars, ganache icing, modeled fondant

0127 Cake Slice: white marshmallow fondant, hand-painted sugarpaste flowers

0128 Not So Pink Valentines: handmade sugarpaste roses, sugarpaste flowers with flower cutters

0129 Black & Pink Cookies: rolled fondant, cutter & veiner, edible luster dust

0130 Cuor di Lampone: dark ganache, sugarpaste flowers

0131 Rolled Chocolate Sugar Cookies with Blossoms: piped royal icing, fondant decoration

0132 Peacock Feather Cake: rolled pearlized peacock blue fondant, hand-cut fondant peacock feathers, disco gold glitter royal icing

0133 Kiwi Fluff Cake: chocolate cake with whipped cream, kiwi & blueberries

0134 Heart Large Cupcakes: candy clay heart, sprinkles

0135 Green Flowers Cupcake: fresh flowers on meringue frosting

0136 Lime Green: rolled fondant, ribbon roses

0137 Pistachio Pistachio: pistachio buttercream swirl, fresh toasted pistachios

0138 Eggs & a Teapot: royal icing, edible paint

0139 Lily Cupcake Tree: light pink dyed frosting swirl trimmed in fine crystal sugar, gumpaste pink lily

0140 Catharine: fondant, buttercream, sugar crystals

0141 Red & Pink Rose Cupcakes: chocolate fondant, handmade fondant details

0142 Pink Cameo Cake: fondant, piping, sculpting

0143 Pink Daisy Cake: rolled fondant, flower paste daisies, sparkle powder

0144 Butterfly Cookies: royal icing

0145 My Love: rolled fondant, fondant cutouts & hand-painted details

0146 Vintage Rose: molded sugarpaste rose, luster dusts

0147 Feather Blossom: embossed fondant circle cutout topped with blossom & feather, buttercream

0148 Yellow Dress: fondant, gumpaste, piped royal icing, flooding, luster painting, gumpaste flowers

0149 Sunflower: flower cutter

0150 Pansies in a Pot: ceramic pots filled with cake & buttercream icing, handmade & painted gumpaste pansies

0151 My Gold Roses: rolled fondant, air-brushed plastic chocolate roses

0152 Saffron Cupcake: fondant decorations

0153 Spring Daisy: rolled fondant, royal icing

0154 Sugar Hearts: sugar cookies

0155 Crystal Cake: rolled fondant, sugar crystals

0156 Rebecca's 21st Birthday Cupcakes with Peacock Tail: embossed fondant

0157 The First Snowfall: piped buttercream, sugar pearls, edible glitter, rolled & punched fondant

0158 Vintage Heart: white chocolate fondant, silicone mold

0159 Elisabett's Cake: fondant, flower paste & cutters

0160 Salvatore & Antonia's 60th Anniversary Cupcakes: buttercream, silver dragee, edible glitter, fondant photo, royal icing beadwork

0161 Bunch of Flowers: fondant, all silk flowers

0162 Purple Mauve Roses, Cymbidium Orchids, Green Dendrobium Orchids: gumpaste on rolled fondant

0163 Happy Birthday JLO: modeled fondant, painted gel colourings

0164 Lavender & Cream Cupcakes: buttercream, handmade fondant sugar roses

0165 Lilac Cookies: sugar cookie, brush embroidery, royal icing

0166 Indian Summer Cupcake Collection: chocolate ganache swirl, sugarpaste flowers & shapes

0167 Purple & Lime Blooms: embossed fondant circle cutout topped with handmade blooms, buttercream

0168 Autumn Wedding Cake: painted rolled fondant, buttercream swirl with hand-painted fondant disk

0169 Peach Butterflies: ganache, panels & curls, flooded chocolate design

0170 Fall Nature Cake: rolled fondant, painted with stamps & stencils

0171 India: fondant

0172 Autumn Bird Cake: painted rolled fondant

0173 Teapot Cake: fondant, hand painting

0174 Silver Snowflake Bouquet: fondant, texture mats, black food color pen, pearl dust

0175 Tall Mini Cake: choclate wrap, two-tone curls

0176 Geraldine Dahlke Flower: cake bite with flower paste flower

0177 Lovely Malteaser: piped whipped cream, malteaser chocolate topper

0178 Oreo Cookie: piped Oreo whipped cream, oreo cookie

0179 Chocolate Zigzag: piped buttercream, piped chocolate

0180 Nina: rolled fondant, hand painted

0181 Plaid Petit Fours: poured fondant, airbrushed design

0182 The Painted Flower Cake: hand-painted rolled fondant

0183 Poppy Cake: rolled fondant, chocolate, poppy seed

0184 Flowered Petit Fours: marzipan, candied flowers

0185 Flower Cupcake: piped buttercream

0186 Frangipani Cupcake: chocolate buttercream, modelling paste frangipani & leaf

0187 Doin' the Polka: fondant, sugar ribbons

0188 Embossed Rose: embossed rolled fondant with purchased rose

0189 Vanilla Birthday Cupcake with Pink Flower: fondant flowers

0190 Special Occasion Cake: embossed rolled fondant, sugar pearls, satin ribbon

0191 Flower Petal Cupcake: vanilla buttercream, rose petal

0192 White Chocolate Raspberry Cupcake: piped Italian buttercream

0193 Cookies for Miranda: royal icing, painted with food coloring

0194 Cutting Cake with Roses: fondant roses, piped buttercream

0195 Strawberries & Cream: piped buttercream, drizzled strawberry topping, fresh strawberries

0196 O'Cake Balls: chocolate-covered cake & gumpaste flowers

0197 Mini Wedding Cakes: rolled fondant, fondant flowers, piped royal icing

0198 Croatian Theme 50th Anniversary: fondant, handmade fondant decorations, butttercream-iced cupcakes, handmade decorations & ribbons

0199 Daisy Mini Cake: marshmallow fondant

0200 Daisy Cupcake: rolled fondant, flower cutter

0201 Red & Teal Mini Cake: marshmallow fondant, silver dragee

0202 Flower Cupcakes: fondant roses & other handmade flowers

0203 Lemon Raspberry Cupcake (& Friends): raspberry jam, lemon buttercream, fresh raspberry

0204 Ode to Michael Miller: fondant, edible images, gumpaste flower

0205 Petit Fours: glazed with icing

0206 Sunflower Cake: rolled fondant with piped sunflowers

0207 Yellow Hearts with Rose: sugar cookie, flooded & piped royal icing, pearl dragees, fondant roses

0208 Yellow Daisy: fondant circles topped with handmade fondant daisy

0209 Gold Flower Appliqué Cake: piped royal icing, hand-molded gumpaste, rolled fondant

0210 Calla Lily Cake: rolled fondant, gumpaste calla lilies & draping

0211 Lily Cupcakes: rolled fondant

0212 Blue Flower Cake: vanilla fondant, fondant flowers

0213 A Flutter of Snow Cakes: piped royal icing, rolled & punched fondant

0214 Lily & Rose Mini Cake: vanilla fondant, gumpaste, petal dust, rose & heart cutters

0215 Chocolate Cherry Coconut Cupcake: fondant flower

0216 Wedgewood Cookie Platter: royal icing

0217 Cameo Blue: molded cameo face, fondant background

0218 Quilling Flowers Cake: fondant

0219 Summer Bees: fondant

0220 Peacock Cake: painted rolled fondant, hand-molded fondant, cream cheese with grapes

0221 Mini Cakes for Cake Tasting: rolled fondant, buttercream, fruit icing, Bavarian cream, gumpaste, petal dust

0222 Mini Mini Flower Cupcakes: poured fondant, piped royal icing

0223 Petit Flower Cookies: royal icing, piped icing flower, brush embroidery

0224 Yellow & Purple Petit Fours: poured fondant, airbrushed design, pressed sugar decoration

0225 Sweet Romance: honey cookies, royal icing, hand-painted luster dust

0226 Butterfly Peaks: piped buttercream, handmade fondant decorations

0227 Spring Is in the Air: rolled fondant

0228 Orange Blossom Cookies: original design on edible sugar paper

0229 Rose Cake: painted rolled fondant

0230 Cupcakes for My Soulmate: fondant, handmade fondant flowers

0231 Topiary Rose Cookies: rolled fondant textured & modeled, brushed luster dusts

0232 Chocolate Roses: chocolate mousse cake, chocolate roses & sides

0233 Flower Cookie: royal icing, brush embroidery

0234 Butterfly Flutter: embossed fondant disk, pink sprinkles, butterfly & mini daisies made with cutters

0235 Rose Cupcake: butterfly patchwork cutter, leaf cutter, luster dust

0236 Rolled Cupcakes: white rolled chocolate paste, handmade sugarpaste flowers

0237 Shimmer Flower Mini Cake: marshmallow fondant, shimmer dust

0238 Trio of Coffee & Chocolate: piped buttercream, sweets for decoration

0239 Wedding Anniversary Cookie: fondant

0240 Hazelnut Praline Cupcakes: buttercream

0241 Black & Beige: fondant flowers & decorations

0242 Sugarflower: flower paste sugar flowers

0243 Another Dotty Cake!: ganache, chocolate detail

0244 Simone: white chocolate ganache, rolled chocolate shards

0245 English Roses Cupcakes: buttercream, handmade fondant sugar roses & leaves, edible glitter, piped royal icing hearts

0246 Mini Cakes: fondant

0247 Spring Cupcakes: handmade fondant roses & various flowers, large pearl dragees

0248 Blue Cake: buttercream frosting, piping

0249 Heart Cupcakes: fondant, heart cutters

0250 Blue Painted Cake: fondant, hand painting

0251 Spider Daisies: sponge-painted fondant, fondant spider daises, gumpaste dragonflies, hand-painted stems & leaves

0252 Butterfly Laces: piped white chocolate butterfly, veiner flower mold

0253 Paisley Cookies: sugar cookies, royal icing flooding, piping

0254 Chocolate Lovers!: chocolate & fondant toppings, some handmade, some purchased

0255 Roses are Red: chocolate curls & shavings, ganache & buttercream icings, molded chocolate

0256 Scrumptilicious: chocolate ganache, buttercream

0257 Red-Tipped Cupcake: vanilla buttercream with red edging

0258 Chocolate Garden: dark ganache, red handmade marshmallow fondant flowers

0259 Caramel Apple Cupcakes: piped caramel, apple peel spiral

0260 Coconut Cream Pie Cupcake: coconut buttercream, coconut cream, fresh coconut

0261 Birthday Butterflies: gumpaste figures, painted with petal dusts

0262 Sweet Potato Pie: sweet potato buttercream filled with a scoop of sweet potato pie, streusel topping

0263 Black & Gold Heart Cupcakes: fondant, texture mats, gold dust

0264 Swayed Petit Fours: poured fondant, airbrushed luster, writing gel, milk chocolate, dragées

0265 Crowned with Copper Jewelry Cake: stencils, cake jewelry

0266 Bib & Rattle Cupcakes: rolled fondant

0267 Cupcake Babies: piped buttercream, piped royal icing, hand painting

0268 Screaming Baby Baby Shower Cake: lemon buttercream, rolled fondant

0269 Baby Shower Cake: rolled fondant

0270 Baby Shower: piped royal icing

0271 Baby Blocks: rolled fondant, simple gum paste flower

0272 Baby Booties Cake: fondant-covered cake with gumpaste booties

0273 Baby Girl Cookies: royal icing

0274 Booties: royal icing

0275 It's a Girl!: buttercream & sugarpaste

0276 Baby Cupcake Onesie: honey cookies royal icing

0277 Twin Baby Cookie: fondant, hand decorated

0278 Bow Cupcake: handmade sugarpaste bow, piped buttercream

0279 Baby Shower Cookie: fondant

0280 Baby Cookie: fondant

0281 Baby Shower Petit Fours: poured fondant, airbrushing, white chocolate details

0282 Baby's Breath: embossed fondant disk with molded dragonfly, ribbon, feet & bee

0283 Baby Shower: rolled fondant, silicone molds

0284 Building Block Cupcakes: piped buttercream with hard candy décor

0285 Butterfly Romance: buttercream, gelatin butterflies, fondant flowers

0286 Baby Handprint Cake: rolled fondant, handprint

0287 Butterfly Baby: piped buttercream, piped white chocolate butterflies

0288 Blue & Green Painted Cookies: painted run sugar

0289 Baby Feet: baby feet mold

0290 Sleepy Bear: rolled fondant, piped royal icing

0291 It's a Girl: Baby Shower Cake: buttercream finish, fondant detail work, gumpaste detail work

0292 It's a Boy: piped royal icing

0293 It's a Girl: Duckie Shower Cake: buttercream finish, fondant detail work

0294 Babyblue Cherub: fondant

0295 Baby Bibs: embossed fondant bibs, laced with fondant handmade ribbon, molded baby toppers

0296 Collegiate Onesie Cookie: sugar cookie, flooded & piped royal icing, hand-painted stripes, fondant monogram

0297 Baby Shower Cake: fondant, gumpaste girl

0298 Alexander: hand molding/marzipan, rolled fondant, gumpaste flowers

0299 Shower: fondant, gumpaste

0300 Baby Boy: fondant, gumpaste figure modeling, pastillage modeling, piped royal icing, hand painting, embossing

0301 Teddy Bears & Ice Cream: royal icing, handmade fondant decorations

0302 Animals & Flowers Cake: chocolate cake, moldable chocolate wrap, handmade fondant animals & flowers, fabric ribbon

0303 Butterfly Birthday Cake: rolled fondant, buttercream, dried fondant butterflies on wires

0304 Teddylicious Birthday Cake: rolled fondant, hand-sculpted figure

0305 Perfume Bottle Cookie for Émilie: royal icing

0306 1st Birthday: rolled fondant

0307 Monkey Baby Cake: buttercream, fondant embellishments

0308 Birthday Cake: rolled fondant

0309 Baby Bootie & Butterflies: royal icing butterflies, sugarpaste shoe, rolled fondant, airbrush

0310 Crocodile Cupcake: rolled fondant

0311 Tiger Cupcake: rolled fondant

0312 Monkey Cupcake: rolled fondant

0313 Elephant Cupcake: rolled fondant

0314 Jungle Animals: rolled fondant

0315 Fireman Cookie: Hydrant: sugar cookie, flooded & piped royal icing, hand painted with edible marker

0316 Fireman Cookie: Fire truck: sugar cookie, flooded & piped royal icing, hand painted with edible marker

0317 Fire Truck Cake: rolled fondant

0318 Fireman Cookie: Dalmation: sugar cookie, flooded & piped royal icing

0319 Fireman Cookie: Hat: sugar cookie, flooded & piped royal icing, hand painted with edible marker

0320 Good Old Hoe Down Birthday Cake: buttercream finish, fondant detail work, gumpaste detail work

0321 Train, Plane & Car Baby Shower: rolled fondant, hand-cut embellishments

0322 Western First Birthday Cake: buttercream finish, fondant detail work, gumpaste topper

0323 Carnival Time: buttercream & sprinkles, real cotton candy, circus peanuts, plastic clown

0324 Dancing Circus Elephant Cookie: all rolled fondant, painted with corn syrup for shine, borders of extruded fondant

0325 Jojo's Circus Cookies: fondant-covered cookie

0326 Jack-in-the-Box Cupcake: extensive modeling

0327 Circus Elephant Birthday Cake: buttercream finish base, fondant finish elephant, fondant detail work, rice cereal elephant head

0328 Summer Days: hand-drawn & cut, rolled fondant, piped buttercream

0329 Princess Castle: rolled fondant, piped royal icing

0330 Little Pets: handmade head mold, gumpaste

0331 Little Rose Fairy: fondant

0332 Flowers for Kate: frosting, piped royal icing

0333 Ballet Cupcakes: fondant, fondant decorations

0334 Piggy on a Stick: rolled sugar cookie on a stick, piped & flooded royal icing, edible pen & fondant embellishment

0335 Ewok Cupcake: rolled fondant

0336 Master Yoda Cupcake: rolled fondant

0337 C-3PO Cupcake: rolled fondant

0338 R2-D2 Cupcake: rolled fondant

0339 Spaceship Cupcakes with Aliens: fondant

0340 Alien Invasion: rolled sugar cookie on a stick, piped & flooded royal icing, edible pen & fondant embellishment, cupcake with buttercream frosting

0341 Jordan's Rocket & Planets Birthday Cupcakes: fondant, painting

0342 Cowboy Baby Cake: fondant

0343 Puppy Cupcake: piped buttercream grass, modeled fondant

0344 Sweet Teddy Bear: piped chocolate ganache, handmade dusted gumpaste teddy bear

0345 Bears & Blocks Cake: rolled fondant

0346 Pony Mad: hand-modeled pony heads

0347 Pirate Cookies: fondant, dusting powders, food color pens

0348 Mom & Daughter Cupcakes: rolled fondant

0349 Alice's Madhatter Cupcake: extensive modeling

0350 Daisycakes: fondant, royal icing

0351 Fun Giraffes: buttercream, cutout fondant giraffe

0352 Fairy Garden: fondant fairy with embossed wings, grass piping nozzle

0353 Puff the Magic Dragon Cake: painted rolled fondant, modeled sugar paste

0354 Sweet Treats Cookie Challenge Nursery Rhyme Entry: rolled fondant, piped royal icing, painted gel coloring

0355 Birthday Cake for Little Girl: mud-cake, fondant

0356 Teddy Bear Picnic: rolled fondant, modeled figures

0357 Fly Away: piped royal icing

0358 Ballerina Slipper Cookies: rolled sugar cookie, freehand royal icing

0359 Little Girl Christening Cake: rolled fondant finish, royal icing detail work, royal icing butterflies

0360 Pink & White Girly Cake: fondant, sanding sugar, gumpaste

0361 Camryn Rose: piped buttercream on cupcakes, handmade fondant roses, butterflies & flowers made with cutters

0362 Teddy Bears: rolled fondant, textured rolling pin, modeled gumpaste

0363 Butterfly Cookies: rolled fondant with piped icing & glitter

0364 Cookie Doll Cupcakes: buttercream skirt, decorated cookie body

0365 Tea & Tiers for Mia: fondant, royal icing

0366 Benny: fondant, gumpaste accents

0367 Baby Prince Bath Time: rolled fondant, marshmallow cream

0368 American Indian Cookies: hand-rolled fondant

0369 Jack's Big Music Show Cake: rolled fondant, handmade fondant figures

0370 Jungle Theme Christening Cake: rolled fondant

0371 Fireman Cupcakes: two-toned, star-piped buttercream icing, piped royal icing fire & water, gumpaste fireman

0372 Fulanitas: buttercream, gumpaste decorations

0373 Queen of Hearts: fondant

0374 Baby Shower Butterfly Cookie Favor: rolled fondant, piped royal icing

0375 Princess Castle: marshmallow fondant, gumpaste flowers, royal icing

0376 Princess Cupcake: buttercream, fondant crown

0377 Fit for a Princess: fondant, buttercream, sugar crystals

0378 Tea Party for One: fondant, gold luster paint

0379 Ellie: fondant, gumpaste bear

0380 Camping Cake: rolled fondant, gumpaste

0381 Gumnut Cottage: modelled rolled fondant & modeling paste, piped royal icing

0382 Spider Cookie: sugar cookie, piped royal icing, sanding sugar, nonpareils

0383 Lizard Cookie: sugar cookie, piped royal icing, sanding sugar, nonpareils

0384 Little Miss Muffet: piped buttercream, piped royal icing, hand painting

0385 Ryden's 1st Birthday: piped royal icing

0386 Party Cows Barn Cake: hand-colored rolled fondant, hand-modeled animals

0387 Caterpillar: buttercream, mini muffins

0388 Monkey Cake: hand-piped vanilla & banana buttercream

0389 Domo-kun Cupcake: brown sprinkles, M&M eyes, fondant teeth & mouth

0390 Duck Cupcakes: hand-modeled fondant

0391 Peppa's Picnic: rolled fondant, hand-molded fondant figures, fondant cutouts

0392 Wild West Cookies: royal icing

0393 Piggy Birthday Cupcakes: rolled fondant, hand-sculpted figures

0394 Look Out: rolled fondant textured & modeled, painted gel coloring

0395 Baa Baa Black Sheep: piped royal icing

0396 Jolly Pirate Cupcake: extensive modeling

0397 Monkey See, Monkey Do Jungle Animal Baby Shower Cake: buttercream, fondant detail work, gumpaste detail work

0398 Choo Choo Cupcake: rolled fondant

0399 Sheep In Love: rolled fondant, handmade chocolate dusted roses, modeled chocolate figurine, royal icing

0400 Lisa Fairy: handmade fondant fairy & accessories, piped grass

0401 Fairy Kingdom: fondant, modeling paste, flower paste & cutters, powdered color

0402 Building Birthdays: printed cupcake toppers, fondant decorations

0403 Hope's Carousel Cake: chocolate cake, buttercream frosting, handmade fondant flowers, 500 handmade fondant roses on top

0404 Flower Cupcake: fondant

0405 In the Night Garden: modeling & details with sugarpaste & modelling paste

0406 Lovey Bears Cupcakes: modeling paste, rolled fondant

0407 Space Cupcake: Rice Krispies Treats, fondant, extensive modeling

0408 Christening Cake: rolled fondant, fondant nest, feather bird

0409 O'Birthday Party: rolled fondant

0410 4th Birthday Cupcake: sponge cake, silver balls

0411 Little Princess Palace: modelled rolled fondant & modeling paste

0412 Bear Cake: rolled fondant, modeled bear

0413 Baby in the Bath Cake: rolled fondant, hand-molded baby & bath toys

0414 If I Had an Aeroplane: rolled fondant, fondant cut-outs

0415 Candle Cookie: Little Girl with Braces: piped royal icing

0416 Circus Cake: fondant, gumpaste embellishments

0417 Princess Cupcake: piped frosting, fondant decorations

0418 Melia's 1st Birthday Cake: rolled fondant, handmade gumpaste flowers & ladybugs, handmade rice paper butterflies

0419 Mad Hatter's Tea Party: hand-painted fondant & buttercream toppers

0420 Frog Prince: hand sculpted

0421 Princess Castle Cake: rolled fondant

0422 Star Wand Cookies: sugar cookie, piped royal icing, silver dragees

0423 Baby Shower Surprise Box: fondant decorations & figures

0424 100 Days: fondant, sculpted fondant, hand painting/drawing

0425 First Comunión: rolled fondant, cold porcelain

0426 Will's Christening: buttercream, handmade fondant topper, piped royal icing

0427 First Communion: handmade fondant & sugar flowers, piped royal icing

0428 Pastel Animal Cookies: run sugar iced, flocking with sugar

0429 Fairy Cookie Bouquets: painted run sugar

0430 Christening Angels: piped royal icing

0431 Girl's First Communion: piped royal icing

0432 Christening Crosses: piped royal icing

0433 Kayla's Birthday Cookies: fondant, piped royal icing

0434 Ballerina Cake: fondant, molded fondant ballerina slippers

0435 Tinkerbell Cake: buttercream icing, fondant decorations

0436 Fairy Cottage: modelled rolled fondant & modeling paste

0437 Three Years Old: piped buttercream, embossed rolled fondant

0438 Kaliya's Birthday Cake Cookies: royal icing

0439 Dancing Mice: fondant, embossing

0440 Christmas Bauble Cookies: sugarpaste, piped royal icing

0441 Christmas Tree with Gold Ornaments Cookie: rolled fondant, patchwork cutter, nonpareils snow

0442 Nutcracker Twins: piped royal icing, hand painting, sugar flocking

0443 Haunted Group Cookie: gingerbread & sugar cookies, royal icing, black sanding sugar, candy embellishments

0444 Flores de Cempasúchil con Calaveritas: piped royal icing

0445 Sparkly Ornaments: rolled sugar cookies, piped & flooded royal icing, sanded sugar

0446 Present Cookies: rolled sugar cookies, piped & flooded royal icing, fondant embellishment

0447 Rudolph Cookies: rolled sugar cookies, piped & flooded royal icing, edible pen, fondant & pretzel embellishment

0448 Fondant Lollies: fondant, food coloring, lollipop sticks

0449 Holiday Garland: mother/daughter created cookies on ribbon

0450 Spooky House: rolled fondant, fondant & flower paste decorations, edible paint

0451 Eco Chic Gingerbread House: gingerbread house covered in fondant with painted detail

0452 Gingerbread Stars: gingerbread & shortbread cookies

0453 Mince Pies Cake: sculpted cake, rolled fondant, hand painting

0454 Thanksgiving Cookie Place Card: royal icing on spice cookie

0455 Christmas Croquembuche: cream puffs, spun sugar

0456 Angry Gingerbread Man: piped royal icing

0457 Stars & Stripes: fondant, gumpaste

0458 Chocolate Cupcake with Blue Star: ganache, chocolate curls, rolled fondant cutout

0459 Christmas Cupcakes: smooth fondant with fondant decoration

0460 Cacao-Star Cookies: cacao dough

0461 Nesting: toasted coconut on buttercream

0462 Hanukkah, Dreidel Side & Menorah Side: fondant, hand painting

0463 Knock Knock Cookies: original design on edible sugar paper

0464 Nativity Scene: buttercream, handmade fondant toppers

0465 Sweet Vampire: piped royal icing

0466 Fourth of July Cupcake: piped buttercream

0467 Love Birds: edible sugar paper

0468 Three-Color Mint Patties: handmade mint patties

0469 Red Sleigh: piped royal icing, hand painting, sugar flocking

0470 Fourth of July Fireworks: piped royal icing

0471 Easter Egg Cookie Collection: honey cookies, royal icing, inspired by Ukrainian Easter eggs

0472 Snowman Cupcake: hand-modeled fondant

0473 My Funny Valentine: gumpaste fantasy flowers, piped royal icing hearts

0474 Young Santa Cookie: rolled fondant, edible gel color, crimped

0475 Valentine Silhouette Couple: sculpted & extruded rolled fondant

0476 Red Love Cookies: rolled fondant, embossed

0477 Christmas Petit Fours: frosting & rolled fondant

0478 Oooops, Santa: sugarpaste Santa's legs

0479 Topsy Turvy Candy Cane: chocolate transfer sheets & silicone mats

0480 Candy Cane Cookies: rolled sugar cookies, piped & flooded royal icing, red licorice lace

0481 Saint Valentine's Cookies: piped royal icing

0482 Valentine Wedding Cookies: stenciling on sugarpaste

0483 Christmas Chocolate Box: embossed moldable chocolate, material bow, handmade fondant flowers

0484 Christmas Tree: one big buttercream swirl

0485 Rose Heart Cookie: royal icing

0486 Candle Cakes: buttercream, coconut, candies & other embellishments

0487 Holly Cupcake: poured fondant glaze, piped royal icing, fondant leaves

0488 Vintage Christmas Cookies: wafer paper, royal icing, fondant flowers

0489 Witches Hat: buttercream

0490 Happy Halloween: buttercream swirl, fondant pumpkin

0491 Pumpkin Place Setting: fondant & food pens

0492 Halloween Petit Fours: frosting & rolled fondant

0493 Halloween Witch Cupcake: buttercream swirl, witch made from homemade silicone mold & lightly airbrushed with black to mute colors

0494 Pumpkins in Disguise: rolled fondant, buttercream

0495 Witch Hat Cupcakes: gold luster dust, jimmies

0496 Monster Heads Cookies: flood-iced rolled fondant, royal icing piping

0497 Pumpkin Patch Critters: royal icing

0498 Pumpkin Pete: hand-molded fondant, gumpaste sculpting

0499 Christmas Penguins: piped royal icing, sprinkles, disco dust

0500 Christmas Kids: piped royal icing

0501 Halloween Birthday Gift: piped royal icing, sprinkles

0502 Big Calaverita: piped royal icing

0503 Halloween Cat: piped royal icing, sprinkles

0504 Santa's Face: piped royal icing, sprinkles, disco dust

0505 Snowflakes Snowmen: piped royal icing, sprinkles, disco dust

0506 Gingerbread Centerpiece, Tree: honey cookies, royal icing, sanding sugar, sugar hearts

0507 Sculpted Heart Cake: rolled fondant

0508 All the Trimmings: royal icing, fondant flowers, edible glitter

0509 I Heart Cupcakes: buttercream

0510 M Loves G Cupcake: modeling on cupcake

0511 Easter Egg Cookie: honey cookie

0512 Chocolate Peppermint: dark chocolate ganache, peppermint buttercream, candy cane crumbles

0513 Easter Bunny Rabbit: fondant, dummy for shop display

0514 Baby Bunny: gumpaste figure modeling, hand painting, fondant, embossing

0515 Easter Cupcakes: fondant

0516 Easter Fondant: fondant & buttercream borders

0517 Easter Bunny Cupcakes: rolled fondant

0518 He Is Risen: royal icing, fondant dove

0519 Easter Egg Cake: rolled fondant, raspberry-filled spongecake

0520 Stocking Cookies: red & white chocolate, chocolate transfer sheets, piped chocolate

0521 Christmas Kittens: rolled fondant

0522 Easter Bunny Cake: hand-modeled fondant, piped buttercream

0523 Christmas Cookie: fondant, hand painted with food coloring

0524 Seasons Greetings: fondant

0525 Happy Little Christmas Elves: rolled fondant handmade sugar figures

0526 Assorted Valentine Cookies: rolled fondant, royal icing

0527 Winter Wonderland of Cookies: rolled fondant, edible glitter

0528 Vintage Easter Cookies: sugar cookies with edible images

0529 Shimmer Heart Swirl: embossed fondant circle cutout, buttercream

0530 Spooky 13th Birthday: buttercream & handmade decorations

0531 Royal Chocolate: piped chocolate buttercream, perfectly placed sprinkles

0532 Poinsettia Print: royal icing

0533 Ghost Cupcakes: candy clay, royal icing eyes

0534 Christmas Tree: ganache, piped chocolate

0535 Halloween Wedding: fondant, gumpaste, piped royal icing, airbrushing, marzipan, sugarveil

0536 Easter Basket: piped buttercream flowers, chocolate eggs

0537 Christmas Tree Cookie with Red & Blue Ornaments: rolled fondant, garland made from cutting & lifting curved lines

0538 Witches Hats: melted chocolate, ice cream cones

0539 My Little Valentine: rolled fondant, heart & flower cutter

0540 Christmas Mini Cupcakes: modeling on minicupcakes

0541 Calaveritas: handmade fondant decorations

0542 Personalized Christmas Cupcakes: rolled fondant, hand-sculpted figures

0543 Easter Parade: embossed fondant disk, handmade chicks with fondant ribbons

0544 Mice on Cheese: rolled fondant, modeled mice

0545 Lion Dance Cake: sculpted cake, rolled fondant, hand painted

0546 Sideways Halloween Silhouette Cake: cake stacked on side, fondant moon, buttercream transfer silhouette

0547 Mini Bundt Jack O'Lanterns: two stacked & filled mini bundt cakes, rolled fondant, airbrushed highlights

0548 Vintage Halloween Cookies: royal icing

0549 Korny Cookie: flood-iced rolled fondant, royal icing piping

0550 Rudolph Cupcake: hand-modeled fondant, piped dark chocolate antlers

0551 Halloween Cookies: piped royal icing

0552 Christmas Trees: rolled fondant, stencil, luster dust

0553 Christmas Cupcake: fondant

0554 Mini Ornament Cakes: hand-painted, rolled fondant

0555 Christmas Stocking Cake or Cookie Overlay: sculpted rolled fondant

0556 Christmas Cookie Set: fondant, hand painted with food coloring

0557 EEK!: piped royal icing

0558 Christmas Cheer: rolled fondant, gumpaste poinsettias & bow loops, fondant holly leaves & berries

0559 Sweetheart Cupcakes: quilt embosser, heart cutter, dragees

0560 Christmas Cupcakes: rolled fondant, handmade fondant decorations

0561 Christmas Cake: fondant

0562 Christmas Cupcake: rolled fondant, gel icing

0563 White Christmas: honey cookies, royal icing

0564 Wreath Cookie: rolled fondant, leaves & holly from mold

0565 Holly Jolly Christmas: chocolate decorations, buttercream

0566 Christmas Gift Cake: fondant, piped royal icing, gumpaste

0567 Christmas Cakes: fondant, dragees

0568 Happy Holidays Tweet Cookies: original design on edible sugar paper

0569 Old Santa Head Cookie: rolled fondant, edible gel color, edible luster dust

0570 Dimestore Santa & Reindeer Cookie Sculptures: colored dough

0571 Chinese New Year Cake: airbrushed buttercream, fondant accents, handmade fondant dragon

0572 Swirl Heart Cookie: rolled fondant, royal icing, nonpareils

0573 Valentine's Cookie & Sugar Cube: royal icing

0574 Santa Face Cookies: royal icing with sparkling sugar

0575 Mini Sample Ornaments: hand-painted, rolled fondant

0576 Winter Wonderland Cupcakes: snowflake cutters, luster dust

0577 Black & White Heart: sponge cake with icing

0578 Christmas Cupcake: snowflake-embossed fondant

0579 Ivory Reindeer Cookie: gingerbread cookie, royal icing, sanding sugar, candy embellishments

0580 Ivory Santa & Sleigh Cookie: gingerbread cookie, royal icing, sanding sugar, candy embellishments

0581 Ice-Candle Cake: rolled fondant, embellishments

0582 Candy Cake: rolled fondant, royal icing to attach the candy

0583 Co Co Coconut: buttercream, fondant

0584 Magical Butterfly Garden: buttercream, fondant

0585 Caterpillar Cupcake: buttercream, sugarpaste, fondant

0586 Wardrobe Cookies: rolled fondant

0587 Chick Hangout: ganache, candy, hand painting

0588 Andy Warhol-Inspired Cake: fondant, hand painted according to an Andy Warhol dessert drawing, sugarpaste heart

0589 Colors in Bloom: piped royal icing

0590 Daisies: piped royal icing

0591 Smilin' Starfish: piped royal icing

0592 Flower Cookies in Vase: sugar cookies, flooded & piped royal icing, sanding sugar

0593 Whimsical Flowers: piped royal icing

0594 Irene: fondant "shifted" squares with bold floral pattern

0595 Where the Buffalo Roam: piped royal icing, hand painting/drawing

0596 Brownie Daisies: brownies, royal icing, M&M candies

0597 Crazy Colors: rolled fondant, piped royal icing

0598 Squirrel, Owl & Mushroom Cookies: piped royal icing

0599 Snowball: piped royal icing

0600 Soccer Ball: piped royal icing

0601 Frog Cupcakes: rolled fondant, handmade fondant frogs

0602 18th Birthday: fondant, fondant decorations

0603 Bread & Butterfly: hand-modeled fondant figures

0604 Snail Cookie Pop: royal icing

0605 Butterfly Cookies: sugar with royal icing

0606 Bunch o' Grapes: piped royal icing

0607 Stepping Out!: molded shoe, pearls, & double hearts with mini dragees & white shimmer

0608 Butterfly Cookie: royal icing flood, royal icing marbleizing, sparkling sugar dip

0609 Spring Cupcakes: pumpkin cupcakes with vanilla cream cheese frosting, dipped in sanding sugars, fondant flower

0610 Purple Minis: rolled fondant, flower cutter

0611 Sparkly Tea Party Cookies: piped royal icing, disco dust

0612 Chocolate Contrast: Pastillage elements, piped frosting

0613 Fashion Cookie: fondant, hand painted with food coloring

0614 Flower Fest: modeled fondant, ganache & chocolate slabs

0615 Garden of Flowers Cookies: rolled fondant, royal icing

0616 In Bloom: blossom made with medium carnation cutter, glued onto leaf

0617 Chili Pepper Cookies: royal icing

0618 Orange Garden: rolled fondant, flower cutter

0619 Summer Flip Flops: hand-modeled fondant, embossed fondant

0620 Owl Cookies: sugar cookie, flooded & piped royal icing, sanding sugar

0621 Owl Cookies: piped royal icing

0622 Spring Mini Collection: rolled fondant, royal icing

0623 Birdie Cake: buttercream icing, gumpaste & fondant embellishments

0624 Birdhouse Cookie: fondant

0625 Cake Furniture: royal icing, assorted candies, white chocolate disks

0626 Watering Can Garden Cake: fondant, piped royal icing, gumpaste

0627 Ice Cream Cuppies: handmade fondant ice cream & sundae decorations

0628 Ornate Oak: piped royal icing, sugar flocking

0629 Picnic in the Forest: handmade fondant toppers

0630 Your Average Garden Gnome: rolled & modeled fondant, piped royal icing, painted gel coloring

0631 Topiary Cookies: royal icing

0632 "Owls in Love" cookie favors: royal icing

0633 Mr. & Mrs. Hedge Hog: hand-painted, colored rolled fondant

0634 Spring Cupcakes: chocolate cupcakes, fondant, cutout flowers, sprinkles

0635 Chocolate Cookie Cakes: rolled chocolate sugar cookies, piped royal icing, sprinkles

0636 Snail Cupcake: hand-modeled fondant

0637 Paisley Cupcakes: chocolate-dipped cupcakes, flower & paisleys from white chocolate paste, painting

0638 Tea Set: piped royal icing, hand painting/drawing

0639 Painted Butterfly Cookies: painted rolled fondant

0640 Pink Daisies & Ganache: poured & piped ganache, fondant flowers

0641 Poker-Faced Cats: rolled fondant, hand-molded fondant figures, fondant cut-outs, embossing, hand painting

0642 Mah Jong Cookies: hand-rolled fondant with hand painting

0643 Billiard Balls: fondant

0644 21st Casino Cupcakes: frosting, fondant decorations, purchased chocolates

0645 Blackjack Cookies: piped & flooded royal icing, rolled fondant

0646 Mah Jong Mini Cupcakes: buttercream, fondant

0647 Snowmen with Falling Snow Cookies: layered, piped royal icing

0648 Summer Cookies: rolled fondant, royal icing

0649 Pretty Hearts: cutout fondant toppers

0650 Dalarna Horse: royal icing, edible paint

0651 Matrioshka Cake: rolled fondant, painted, embellishments

0652 Licking Cow: "ice cream" scoop of buttercream, fondant, molded modelling paste, sugarpaste heart

0653 A Partridge in a Pear Tree Cottage: gingerbread house covered in fondant with painted detail

0654 Ladybug Family: figure molding, cake carving, rolled fondant, airbrush

0655 Golf Day Pop!: handmade fondant golf bag, golf clubs & ball, piped grass

0656 Worm & Toadstool: piped buttercream grass, modeled fondant

0657 Dachshund Cupcakes: piped royal icing

0658 Wheatgrass Wedding: textured fondant, handmade gumpaste flowers, petal dust

0659 Colorful Two Tier with Flowers: fondant, food coloring gels

0660 Rainbow Stripe Cookies: sugar cookies, special royal icing, striping technique

0661 Surfboard Cookies: royal icing

0662 Melting Snowman: rolled sugar cookies, piped & flooded royal icing, edible pen & fondant embellishment

0663 Assorted Minis: rolled fondant, royal icing detail, pearl dragees

0664 "A Little Birdie Told Me" cupcakes: buttercream swirl, royal icing piped flowers, hand-shaped fondant birds

0665 Flower Cupcakes: rolled fondant

0666 Oscar Party Cupcakes: chocolate dip, piped buttercream "popcorn," movie candy

0667 County Fair Cookie: sugar cookie, special royal icing, piping

0668 Happy Birthday Swirl: layered colored buttercream, sprinkles

0669 Pool Party Cupcakes: Blueberry Martini, Strawberry Daiquiri, Mudslide: flavored buttercreams

0670 Thank You! Cookies: royal icing, wet-piped stripes & circles, over-piped accents

0671 St. Valentine's Colorful Hearts: piped royal icing

0672 Butterfly Quinceanara Cake: buttercream finish, fondant detail work, silk butterflies

0673 Mehndi-Inspired Cookies: royal icing

0674 Matroyska Cookies: royal icing

0675 Ladybird Cookie Pops: royal icing

0676 Decorated Cookies: royal icing

0677 Let It Snow Cake: rolled fondant, sculpted fondant, piped royal icing, piped chocolate

0678 Penguin Cookie: royal icing, sanding sugar, airbrush

0679 Snowflakes 2007: rolled fondant, royal icing

0680 Star, Moon & Clouds Sugar Cookies: royal icing

0681 Winter Topsy Turvy: buttercream, royal icing snowflakes, impression mat, fondant bows, luster dust

0682 Polka Dot Pretzels: white chocolate-covered pretzel rods

0683 Blue Fish: hand-painted rolled fondant

0684 Climbing Blue Clematis Vine: rolled fondant, royal icing

0685 County Fair Cookie: sugar cookie, royal icing flooding, piping

0686 Flower: buttercream, color flow flower

0687 Rose Swirls: rolled fondant, flower cutter

0688 Lime & Pink Hats & Blossoms: handmade hats, ruffled, flat edged with sprinkles, handmade fondant flowers & details

0689 Cute Worms: handmade fondant toppers

0690 Pink & Orange Cupcakes: flower & leaf cutters, dragees, clay gun

0691 Bumble Bee Love: fondant decorations on vegan cupcakes

0692 Paisley Party Cake: fondant, piped royal icing, airbrush

0693 Tobogan Tower: fondant, hand painting, piped royal icing

0694 Bella Bug Range: fondant, fondant decorations

0695 Bright Light Cupcakes: orange piped buttercream, sprinkles

0696 All Butter, All the Time: shortbread thumbprint cookies, colored lemon icing

0697 Patchwork Quilt Cake: fondant, stamped fondant tiles

0698 Frog Cupcakes: frosting, fondant decorations

0699 Flower Power: fondant, fondant decorations

0700 Cherry Cupcakes: fondant, fondant decorations

0701 Queenie: fondant

0702 Kay Bojensen Monkeys: rolled fondant, fondant & flower paste figures & decorations

0703 Bees Cupcake: buttercream swirl, handmade fondant bees

0704 Mariam's Cupcakes: embossed rolled fondant, fondant ribbon, edible pearls

0705 Mad Hatter Brownie: white chocolate frosting, strawberry preserves

0706 Kids & Snowflakes: royal icing

0707 Bunny Loves Carrot: embossed fondant top, handmade fondant decorations

0708 Ladybugs Cake: rolled fondant, modeling

0709 Pumpkin Cupcakes: nonpareils, hand sculpted

0710 Yin Yang Cupcake: rolled fondant, gumpaste

0711 Chocolate Cake with Autumn Leaves: chocolate fondant, gumpaste leaves

0712 Bright Colored Birthday Cake: rolled fondant, gumpaste, hand-cut name

0713 Pumpkin Cookie Box with Leaves: marbled run sugar iced, fondant-covered cookie box

0714 Harvest Cupcakes: chocolate sprinkles, leaf cutter, daisy cutter, flower center mold

0715 Sports Ball Cupcakes: fondant, texture mats, food color pens

0716 Perk Up Cookie Platter: royal icing on chocolate cookies

0717 Polka Dot Roses & Bow Cake: rolled fondant

0718 Red & Black Cookies: royal icing

0719 Cookie Bug: royal icing, edible paint

0720 Snowman Sugar Cubes: sugar cube, royal icing

0721 Just One Bite: piped buttercream, transparent gel "blood"

0722 Cutwork-Inspired Wonky Cake: sugarpaste, piped royal icing

0723 '50s Cupcakes: fondant decorations brushed with luster dust

0724 Cake Flower: fondant, hand painting, piped royal icing

0725 Fabulous '50s Platter: piped royal icing

0726 Cat Cookie Portraits: piped royal icing

0727 Lovebirds Cake for Two: chocolate mousse, rich fudge frosting

0728 Brunette Hairstyle Cupcake, Brunette Hairstyle Cupcake, Blonde Hairstyle Cupcake, Black Hairstyle Cupcake: rolled fondant

0729 Handbags: 3-D pieces

0730 Birthday Coffee Cookie: fondant

0731 Koala Cupcake: piped buttercream, candy

0732 Butterfly Cookies: sugar cookie, royal icing

0733 Surf's Up Cupcakes: penguin kids' characters handmade from sculpted fondant

0734 Girly Girl Cake: piped buttercream

0735 BEEs!: rolled fondant, simple hand molding

0736 Flower Cookies: piped royal icing

0737 Birds & Bunnies Cupcakes: extensive modeling

0738 Mermaid Cake: fondant with hand-crafted coral & starfish

0739 Heart Cookie: fondant, piped royal icing

0740 Watermelon Cookies: rolled sugar cookies, piped & flooded royal icing

0741 Flower Cake Cut-Outs: rolled fondant decorations

0742 Chickadee Cupcakes: fondant

0743 Spring Daisy Lemon Cupcakes: rolled fondant, piped buttercream

0744 Mini Cupcakes: buttercream, sugar crystals & sweeties

0745 Pink & Green Gift Box Cake: fondant, sugarpaste, fantasy flowers

0746 Beehive Cookie: rolled fondant textured & modeled, painted gel coloring

0747 Labyrinth of Enlightenment: modeled rolled fondant & modeling paste, piped royal icing

0748 Yellow Flower Patch: rolled fondant, flower mold

0749 Yellow Plumeria Cookies: royal icing

0750 Marie Antoinette Dress: honey cookie, royal icing, painted luster dust, inspired by Marie Antoinette

0751 Bumble Bee Cookies: sugarpaste, edible paint

0752 Bumble Bee Cupcake: candy clay bee

0753 S'Mores Cupcakes: marshmallow frosting, graham crackers, piece of chocolate bar

0754 Gerbera Daisies & Butterflies: fondant

0755 Crème Brûlée: piped royal icing

0756 Pink Fizz Jewelry Cake: modeling, modeling paste cutouts

0757 Gabrielle: fondant, printed icing sheet, gumpaste sweets

0758 Other Mother Cake: fondant

0759 Butterfly Cookie: sugar cookie, flooded & piped royal icing, sanding sugar

0760 Cherry Tree Cookies: hand-cut honey cookies

0761 Poodle in Paris Cookie: sugar cookie, royal icing, sanding sugar, satin bow

0762 Little Sweet 16 Cake: fondant icing, gumpaste bow, hand-painted zebra stripes, ribbon roses

0763 Autumn Cookies: piped royal icing, disco dust

0764 Squirrely Scores the Big One: piped royal icing

0765 Bright Daisy Cake: rolled fondant, wired flowers

0766 Owl Cupcakes: piped buttercream, candy

0767 Squirrel & Hedgehog Party: honey cookies

0768 Rabbit Cake: sculpted cake, rolled fondant, hand painted

0769 Daisy Cupcake: buttercream, shell piping, sugar-coated chocolates

0770 Fall Cupcakes: chocolate buttercream icing, fondant embellishments, luster & petal dusts

0771 Blue Flower Cookies: royal icing, nonpareils

0772 Pink & Blue Stars Cupcakes: rolled fondant, piped icing

0773 Thongs Vanilla Sugar Cookies: fondant

0774 Pure Vanilla Cupcakes: piped buttercream, fondant decorations

0775 Farm Cake: fondant

0776 Thank You Cupcake: piped royal icing

0777 Bee & Beehive: buttercream swirl, handmade fondant decorations

0778 Flower Basket Cookies: sugar cookie, royal icing/flowers

0779 Pastel Quilting: transfer sheet on fondant, fondant bow

0780 Kitty Clock House: royal icing

0781 Beehive: Wilton mold, butter cake

0782 Welcome House Cake: hand-modeled rolled fondant

0783 Beehive Cake: fondant, cookie accent

0784 Garden Fans: buttercream & handmade decorations

0785 Mini Snowmen Cake: rolled fondant, fondant decorations

0786 Pink Flower Fun: texture sheet, fondant molding, piped royal icing

0787 Stitched Flower Cake: gumpaste cutouts painted with petal dust, rolled fondant

0788 Magic Roundabout Cupcakes: piped chocolate buttercream, handmade fondant sugar decoration

0789 Bec's Teapots: gumpaste cupcake toppers

0790 Mother's Day Cupcake: rolled fondant

0791 Pink Polka Dots Cake: buttercream icing, fondant decorations

0792 Flower Bouquet: chocolate cookies, royal icing gems, piped royal icing, luster dust

0793 Heart Sugar Cookie Tin: royal icing

0794 Oreo Petit Fours: Oreo cakesters, fondant

0795 Colorful Sandwich Cookies: rolled chocolate sugar cookies, tinted royal icing

0796 Rainbow Cupcake: white cake batter colored with food dyes

0797 Michelle's Signature Cake: rolled fondant

0798 Pot of Gold Cake: rolled fondant, modeling

0799 Rainbow Tea Pot Cookie: piped royal icing

0800 Here's Looking at You: rolled textured fondant, painted gel coloring, brushed luster dusts

0801 Fortune Cookie Cupcakes: candy clay fortune cookies

0802 Whimsical Polka Dot: rolled fondant, airbrush

0803 "I'm a Snow Angel" Cake: rolled & modeled fondant, piped royal icing details

0804 Tea Pot: rolled fondant, textured, silicone molds, pearls, pearl dust

0805 Cookie Jar Cake: rolled fondant, gumpaste for the lid, stencil

0806 Movember Cupakes: rolled fondant

0807 Peace Sign Cookie: rolled fondant with texture mat

0808 Bumble Bee Cupcakes: daisy cutter, flower center mold, circle cutter

0809 Snowman Vignettes: fondant, gumpaste, piped royal icing, airbrushing

0810 Summertime: fondant

0811 Skates: piped royal icing

0812 Snow Dog: piped royal icing

0813 Masculine Birthday Cake: rolled fondant

0814 Bright Stars: cutout fondant toppers

0815 Apple a Day: fondant-covered cookies

0816 Red Kebaya Cake: sculpted cake, rolled fondant, hand painted

0817 It's a Piece of Cake Celebration Cake: rolled fondant finish, fondant detail work

0818 Acid Spring: fondant, cutters

0819 Cupcakes for Julie: fondant, buttercream

0820 Flower Pot Cupcakes: buttercream grass, cookie flower

0821 Love Tree: piped royal icing

0822 Springtime Cupcake Bouquet: rolled fondant, piped buttercream

0823 Roxy: topsy turvy with fondant & gumpaste

0824 Fruit Bowl Cake: sculpted cake, rolled fondant, hand painted

0825 Decorated Cookies: royal icing, fondant flowers & leaves

0826 Sweet Daisy Cake: rolled fondant, gumpaste

0827 Floral Bouquet Cupcake 1: gumpaste, rolled fondant

0828 Pink & Green Cupcakes: swirl embosser, flower, leaf, letter & heart cutters

0829 Dragonfly Cookies: sugar cookies, flooded & piped royal icing

0830 Swedish Dala Horse: royal icing, gingerbread

0831 Lily Pulitzer Cupcakes: vanilla buttercream, fondant flowers & paisley

0832 Allira's Tropical 21st: buttercream, fondant, handmade tropical flowers, cupcakes with buttercream & handmade flowers

0833 Summer Sundaes: buttercream swirl, embossed fondant flowers

0834 Pig Roast Celebration Cake: rolled fondant finish, rice cereal pig

0835 I Love Tokyo: buttercream swirl, fondant & edible cachous

0836 Palm Tree Cookies: butter cookies, glaze icing, fondant coconuts

0837 Japanese-Inspired Birthday Cupcakes: rolled fondant, hand-sculpted figures

0838 A Sushi Dessert: rolled fondant, poured/molded sugarwork, hand painting

0839 Housewarming Cupcakes: fondant, fondant decorations, piped grass frosting

0840 Sports Fans: buttercream & handmade decorations

0841 Floral Bouquet Cupcake 2: gumpaste, rolled fondant

0842 Margarita Cupcakes: custom wrapper, icing, sanding sugar "salt," sugar cookie with royal icing & sanding sugar

0843 Starfish Cookies: hand-rolled fondant with pearl dust & royal icing

0844 Blue Birthday Cupcake: piped chocolate ganache, fondant curls

0845 Embellished Ginger Heart Cookies: rolled fondant

0846 Embellished Ginger Cookies: rolled fondant, piped royal icing

0847 Assorted Minis: rolled fondant, royal icing

0848 Sea Cookies: rolled fondant, hand painting

0849 Royal Icing Butterfly: piped royal icing

0850 Happy Bee Day: rolled fondant, gumpaste

0851 Yellow Hat Box: rolled fondant

0852 Shimmer Heart Cupcakes: rolled fondant, piped royal icing

0853 Bella Bug Range: fondant, fondant decorations

0854 Buttercup Yellow Square with Flowers: fondant, buttercream

0855 Cookie Ring Collection: totally edible 3-D cookie rings, honey cookie, royal icing, fondant sugar diamonds, hand painted with luster dust

0856 O'Peony: rolled fondant, white chocolate pearls, gumpaste peonies

0857 Pink & Delicate: rolled fondant, gumpaste flowers

0858 Art Nouveau Tulip Wedding Cake: art nouveau tulip patchwork cutters

0859 O'Feather: rolled fondant, gumpaste roses, royal icing feather

0860 Fernanda Wedding Cake: rolled fondant, gumpaste flowers

0861 Policeman Wedding Cake: modeling on sugarpaste

0862 Chocolate Scrolls: rolled fondant, chocolate paste

0863 Caroline's Black & White Cake for a French-Themed Wedding: Belgian chocolate ganache under fondant, fresh rose

0864 Pinwheel Cascade Cake: scored gumpaste cutouts painted with petal dust, rolled fondant

0865 Bamboo Plumeria: fondant with etched bamboo & plumeria appliqué

0866 Blossoms & Bow: fondant bow & flowers, piped royal icing

0867 Black & White Wedding: fondant, sugar pearls

0868 Mini Bride & Groom: rolled fondant, pearl finish, sugar pearls

0869 Red Wave Wedding Cake: painting, cake fountain, modeling paste cutouts

0870 Orange & Pink Wedding Cake: fondant, piping, sugarpaste flowers

0871 Pink & Brown Wedding Cake: rolled fondant, piped royal icing, scrolls with silver dragees accents, gumpaste bow topper

0872 Cookie Stack: fondant

0873 Rose Lantern: rolled fondant quilted, handmade swirls

0874 O'Butterfly: rolled fondant, gumpaste flowers & butterflies

0875 Kathleen & Kieran's Engagement Cupcake: fondant

0876 Juliet: fondant with handcrafted stylized flowers

0877 Wedding Birdcage Cake: three tiers on boards inside for easy serving, rolled fondant, piped royal icing

0878 Diamond Ring Cake: fondant, gumpaste embellishments

0879 Double Happiness Wedding Cake: fondant with fondant appliqué

0880 Lambie Cutting Cake: hand-modeled figures

0881 Rosey Wedding Cookie: royal icing, edible paint

0882 Starbrushed: rolled fondant, gold dust stenciling

0883 The Stephanie: rolled fondant, hand-painted double barrel

0884 Elyse: rolled fondant, handmade crystal cake crown

0885 Andrea's Damask Cake: fondant with fondant appliqué, piped buttercream accents

0886 Black/Ivory Hearts: embossed fondant circle cutout topped with heart cutouts/blossoms, buttercream

0887 Bride & Groom Hearts: rolled fondant, embossed

0888 Black & White Cake: fondant, purchased gumpaste flowers, gumpaste drapes & buttons

0889 Molly: rolled fondant, quilted, piped, painted

0890 Organic Cake: white chocolate fondant; gumpaste flower buds, birds & eggs; individually cut gumpaste lace appliqués

0891 Summer Wedding: fondant, embossing

0892 Amanda & Jeff's Wedding Cake: fondant

0893 Pink Ring: piped buttercream, handmade fondant ring

0894 Single Tier Ivory Wedding Cake: rolled fondant, gumpaste flowers topper

0895 Mini Cake: white chocolate fondant, fondant & silk flowers, gumpaste butterfly

0896 Golden Roses Wedding Cake: rolled fondant

0897 Fleur-de-Lis Wedding: rolled fondant, fondant molding

0898 White on White: rolled fondant, gumpaste roses, beads, fondant draping

0899 Here Comes the Cake: fondant drapes, bow & flowers, buttercream frosting & piping

0900 Ball Cake: rolled fondant, gumpaste

0901 August Wedding Cake: buttercream

0902 Crown Princess Wedding: rolled fondant, flower paste roses, fondant panels

0903 White Cake with Sugar Peony: fondant, gumpaste peony, sugar pearls

0904 The Daisy: rolled fondant, fondant cutouts

0905 Ivory Rose Wedding Cake: fondant, applied fondant embellishments, handmade sugar rose

0906 O'White: cream cheese frosting & gumpaste flower

0907 Collection of Mini Cakes: white chocolate fondant, gumpaste butterflies, dragees

0908 Centerpiece Cake: rolled fondant

0909 Centerpiece Cake: rolled fondant, gumpaste flower

0910 Centerpiece Cake: rolled fondant, satin ribbon, gumpaste flower

0911 Centerpiece Cake: rolled fondant, fondant ribbons, gumpaste flowers

0912 Square Mini Cakes: gumpaste gerbera daisies & butterflies

0913 Silver Band Cake: gumpaste bands, piped royal icing, rolled fondant

0914 Cherry Blossom Cake: sugar cookie, royal icing/flowers

0915 Pastel Quilled: smoothed buttercream, fondant rope borders, quilled gumpaste flowers

0916 Wedding Gown Cookie: sugar cookie, royal icing

0917 Purple Flower Cake: sugar cookie, royal icing

0918 Abstract Flower Jewelry Cake: cake jewelry, modeling paste cutouts

0919 Baby Blue & White Wedding Cake: rolled fondant

0920 Love Birds: rolled fondant

0921 Winter Wonderland Wedding Cake: rolled fondant, sugar decoration

0922 M & K Cookies: piped royal icing

0923 Remembrances: piped royal icing

0924 Azaleas Wedding Cake: rolled fondant, piped royal icing, fondant roses

0925 Ivory Bubbles: rolled fondant, fondant-covered dylite balls, pearl finish, gumpaste curls

0926 '70s: marbled fondant, fondant bricks

0927 Wedding Cakes with Fresh Flowers: rolled fondant, fondant band, fresh roses

0928 Gold Love Cake: rolled white fondant, fondant gold bangles hand painted with luster dust

0929 Orange Gerbera Wedding Cake: fondant, quilting, sugarpaste flowers, airbrush

0930 Debbie's Red & Gold Wedding Suitcases: painting, embossing, modeling

0931 Three-Tier Wedding Cake: vanilla buttercream, spring gerbera daisies, ribbon

0932 Just Married in Vegas Cake: buttercream finish, fondant detail work

0933 Woodsy Wedding Cake: chocolate ganache cake wrapped in white chocolate with wood grain transfer

0934 Kristen: hand-painted fondant with handcrafted cherry blossoms

0935 Green Lace, Pearls & Roses: rolled fondant, texture mat, lacy leaf mold, handmade roses & pearls

0936 Bridesmaid Cookies: sugar cookie, royal icing

0937 Engagement Cupcakes: handmade fondant decoration, hearts & owl

0938 White Cake with Flowers: fondant, brushed embroidery

0939 Louise: rolled fondant; gelatin flowers; wired fondant decorations, blossoms & beads; handmade sugar roses dusted with color

0940 Wedding Cupcakes: fondant

0941 Leslie: fondant with color gradations, handcrafted plumerias, & seashells

0942 Kim & David's Wedding Cupcakes: embossed fondant

0943 Daisies & Bow: buttercream with gelatin bow & gumpaste daisies

0944 Indian Patchwork Elephant Wedding Cake: modeling, bas relief, painting

0945 Las Vegas Wonky Wedding Cake: modeling, modeling paste cutouts

0946 Pink & Aqua Wonky Wedding Cake: modeling paste cutouts & cake fountain

0947 Bird House Cake: rolled fondant, hand-painted hand-molded designs

0948 Whimisical Harlequin Wedding Cake: buttercream finish, fondant detail work, super pearl dust painting

0949 40th Wedding Anniversary Cake: painted rolled fondant, modeled sugarpaste

0950 Cliveden Wedding Cake: sugarpaste, modeling paste cut-outs

0951 Preppy 30th Birthday Cake: green fondant, pink gumpaste flowers

0952 Wedding Cake: rolled fondant, fresh roses

0953 Wedding Cookie Set: fondant, hand painted with food coloring

0954 Chocolate Wedding Cake: chocolate rolled fondant, pink piping, tiers separated with fresh flowers

0955 Pastel Cupcakes: rolled fondant

0956 Andrea & Ryan Wedding Cake: rolled fondant, fondant & gumtex bow

0957 Autumn Green Apple Wedding Cake: Swiss buttercream, handmade marzipan apples, fresh orchids

0958 Erica: fondant with vine appliqué & handcrafted hibiscus flower

0959 Green Zari: fondant, gumpaste, piped royal icing, flooding, luster painting, gumpaste flower

0960 Irish-Themed Cake: gumpaste phaleanopsis & cymbidium orchids

0961 Wedding Shower Cake: rolled fondant

0962 Orchid Wedding Cake: gumpaste orchid, painted & petal dusted apple green, red & yellow

0963 Henna-Inspired Cake: buttercream, chocolate designs

0964 Lovebirds Cake: gumpaste cutouts, piped royal icing, rolled fondant

0965 Equal Billing Wedding Cookie: sculpted & extruded rolled fondant

0966 O'Mini Cakes: rolled fondant, gum paste flowers

0967 Wedding Cake: all buttercream, four-tiered basketweave

0968 Hantaran (Engagement) Cake: buttercream, gumpaste roses

0969 Wedding Cake: rolled fondant, fresh flowers

0970 Soft Summer: rolled fondant, gumpaste roses, freesia & hypericum berries

0971 Monogram Unforgettable Purple & Lime Green: original design on edible sugar paper

0972 Gingerbread Bride & Groom: royal icing, dragees

0973 Andrea's Two Birds Cake: fondant with fondant appliqué

0974 Brushed Embroidery Cake: rolled fondant, royal icing brushed embroidery

0975 The Eden: rolled fondant, edible images, hand painted, piped royal icing

0976 Assorted Wedding Cookies: royal icing

0977 Wedding Cupcakes: various buttercream piping

0978 Green-Striped Fondant Cake: fondant, royal icing

0979 Renée & Ben's Topsy Turvy: fondant with fondant appliqué, hand-painted luster dust

0980 Bow Cake: rolled fondant, gumpaste bows, jewelry

0981 Embroidered Wedding Cake: rolled fondant, piped royal icing, fondant calla lilies

0982 Autumn Wedding Cake: rolled fondant with dragees

0983 Turquoise Shower Cake: rolled fondant

0984 Sparkling Ocean Jewelry Cake: cake jewelry, sugarpaste

0985 Textures & Shades of Blue Cake: fondant, gumpaste flowers

0986 Shimmery Winter Cake: gumpaste flowers, criss-crossed scoring on rolled fondant

0987 Sassy Bride Shower Cake: buttercream, fondant detail work, gumpaste topper

0988 "Chintzy" Wedding Cake: fondant, hand painting, piping, handmade sugar rose

0989 Pink Squares Cake: buttercream, flowers

0990 Megan & Juraj's Wedding Cake: rolled fondant, handmade gumpaste peony, royal icing brushed embroidery leaves

0991 Purse Sugar Cookies: piped royal icing, candy clay accents

0992 Wedding Cookie: fondant, hand painted with food coloring

0993 Wedding Cake Cookie Favor: cookies stacked with rolled fondant, sugarpaste flowers

0994 Pretty in Pink: rolled fondant, gumpaste roses, freesia & piped royal icing branches

0995 Zari Embroidery: fondant, gumpaste, piped royal icing, flooding, luster painting

0996 Wedding Cake: rolled fondant, sugar peony & bee detail, piped royal icing

0997 Birthday Mini Cake & Cupcakes: ribbon, butterfly patchwork cutter, hydrangea cutter & veiner, swirl stamp, flower cutters

0998 Bridal Shower Cookies: butter cookies, glaze icing, fondant roses

0999 Two Hearts: sugar cookies

1000 Rococo Bride: fondant, piped royal icing, hand painting, sugar molding, cake carving

contributor directory

Darlene Abarquez, www.make-fabulous-cakes
.com, Canada
darlene@make-fabulous-cakes.com
0536, 0741, 0961

Leoni Abernethy, Happy Cakes, Australia
www.happycakes.com.au
happycakesinfo@gmail.com
0333, 0459, 0602, 0644, 0694, 0697-0700,
0839, 0853

Leisl Adams, Fancimolasses Cake Studio,
Canada
www.brownycakes.blogspot.com
0211

Paula Ames, Cake Creations, Chubbuck, Idaho,
USA
www.amescakecreations.com
cakecreations@cableone.net
0142, 0870, 0929

Laura-Kate Amrhein, www.sweetstirrings.com,
USA,
laurakate1021@gmail.com
0044, 0657, 0802, 0897

Jaime Lynne Anderson, Flutterby Cakes, UK
www.flutterby-cakes.co.uk
jaime_anderson@fsmail.net
0093, 0098, 0124, 0257, 0578

Laura Silvana Astorino, Dulce Materia,
Argentina
laura_77_29@hotmail.com
0425

Aunt Cakes Cookies LLC, Kate Costella, USA
www.auntcakescookies.com
kate@auntcakescookies.com
0368, 0642, 0843

Judy Ayre, Judy Ayre Cakes, Australia
www.judyayrecakes.com
ayrej@me.com
0112, 0232, 0274, 0299, 0330, 0366, 0379,
0757, 0781, 0789, 0823, 0863

Hana Bacova,
www.flickr.com/photos/haniela,
USA
hana_bacova@yahoo.com
0003-0005, 0018, 0072, 0154, 0215, 0225,
0276, 0468, 0471, 0506, 0511, 0563, 0609,
0750, 0760, 0767, 0792, 0855, 0999

Nancy Barinque, Sweet Pudgy Panda, Canada
www.facebook.com/sweetpudgypanda
www.flickr.com/nbarinque
nbarinque@gmail.com
0131, 0272, 0456

Ninotchka Beavers,
www.ninotchkabeavers.com,
USA
ninotchkab@aol.com
0796

Rebecca Bendle, UK
bex.bendle@hotmail.co.uk
0772

Leah Bent, Sweet Icing Bakeshop, USA
www.sweeticingbakeshop.weebly.com
leah.melissa@gmail.com;
sweeticingbakeshop@gmail.com
0199, 0201, 0237

**Better Bit of Butter Cookies,
Christine Mehling**, USA
www.betterbitofbutter.com
christine@betterbitofbutter.com
0028, 0046, 0083, 0084, 0153, 0526, 0622,
0648, 0663, 0684, 0847

Marlyn Birmingham,
www.montrealconfections.com,
Canada
info@montrealconfections.com
0364, 0485, 0573, 0604, 0675, 0680, 0720,
0783, 0820, 0976

Janice Boyd, USA
www.cakesbyjanice.com
ephwoman@netzero.net
0899

Karen Bradley, Cake Believe, USA
www.cakebelieve.net
karen@cakebelieve.net
0063

Renae Bradley,
renaekbradley@gmail.com,
USA
0402, 0461, 0491, 0508, 0518, 0532,
0565, 0691, 0815, 0830

Toni Brancatisano,
www.torteditoni.com,
Italy
toniprev@hotmail.com
0010, 0061, 0103, 0114, 0158, 0161,
0355, 0434, 0513, 0567, 0895, 0907

Janet G. Bravo, The Pretty Little Cake Shop,
USA
www.cupcakesalabravo.blogspot.com
peridotsun@yahoo.com
0039, 0092, 0435, 0682, 0791

Brian & Natalie Braxton, Bratty Cakes, USA
www.brattycakes.com
brattycakes@ymail.com
0049, 0235, 0420, 0495, 0559, 0576, 0690,
0709, 0714, 0808, 0828, 0997

Elisa Brogan,
www.belisacupcakes.com.au,
Australia
belisacupcakes@yahoo.com.au
0024, 0105, 0109, 0234, 0282, 0295, 0352, 0361,
0400, 0543, 0607, 0616, 0655

Gina M. Brown, USA
gmsbrown@aol.com
0133

Yelda Brown, **Fairly Fairy Cakes**, UK
www.fairlyfairycakes.co.uk
yelda@fairlyfairycakes.co.uk
0110

Adriene Brumbaugh, **Shugee's**, USA
www.shugees.com
shugees@sbcglobal.net
0360, 0659, 0706, 0854, 0938

Jennifer Bunce, **The Hudson Cakery**, USA
www.hudsoncakery.com
info@hudsoncakery.com
0184, 0711, 0903, 0951

Taya Burke, **Deliciously Decadent Cake Design**, Australia
www.deliciouslydecadentcakes.webs.com
deliciously_decadent@bigpond.com
0120, 0180, 0244, 0873, 0883, 0884, 0889, 0904, 0975

Gabriela Cacheux, **gabby cupcakes**, Mexico
gabrielacacheux@prodigy.net.mx
0099, 0241, 0301, 0423, 0427, 0541, 0627, 0937, 0940

Cake Hero, Melissa L. Torres, USA
www.cakehero.com
melissa@cakehero.com; cakehero@gmail.com
0268, 0269, 0369

Autumn Carpenter, **Autumn Carpenter Designs**, USA
www.autumncarpenter.com
autumn@countrykitchensa.com
0174, 0263, 0288, 0347, 0428, 0429, 0520, 0692, 0713, 0715

Lauren E. Carrescia, **Dolce Designs**, USA
www.dolcedesigns.com
lauren.carrescia@gmail.com;
dolcedesigns.lc@gmail.com
0290

Lydia C. Carter, **Celene's Cuisine**, USA
www.celenescuisine.com
lydia@celenescuisine.com
0931

Isabel Casimiro, **Pecado dos Anjos**, Portugal
www.pecadodosanjos.net
isabelcasimiro@pecadodosanjos.net
0306, 0308, 0665

Catie, **Catie's Cakes & Cookies**, Australia
www.catiescakesandcookies.blogspot.com
catiescakesandcookies@hotmail.com
0080, 0538, 0806, 0819

Chantilly Cake Designs by Beth Aguiar, Canada
www.flickr.com/photos/cakespace
girlcake2006@yahoo.com
0321, 0413, 0712, 0813, 0860, 0894, 0908-0911, 0927, 0956

Susan Chicola, USA
schicola@si.rr.com
0182, 0210

Suet May Chin, **Sugarcraze Arts**, Malaysia
http://sugarcrazearts.blogspot.com
sugarcraze@hotmail.com;
sugarcrazearts@yahoo.com
0304, 0393, 0542, 0837

Debbie Coetzee, **Choclit D'lites**, South Africa
www.choclitdlites.com;
www.flickr.com/choclit-dlites
choclit.dlites@gmail.com
0169, 0175, 0179, 0238, 0243, 0343, 0437, 0458, 0534, 0656, 0844

Natasha Collins, **Nevie-Pie Cakes**, UK
www.neviepiecakes.com
nevie-pie@hotmail.co.uk
0041, 0168, 0172, 0229, 0353, 0363, 0451, 0639, 0653, 0949

Cookie Creatives by Jennifer, Jennifer J. Burkhart, USA
www.cookiecreatives.com
jennifer@cookiecreatives.com
0066, 0071, 0090, 0165, 0732, 0778, 0914, 0916, 0917, 0936

Cyndi Coon, **Laboratory5** & Sarah Spencer, **Sspencer Studios**, USA
www.laboratory5.com; www.sspencerstudio.com
info@laboratory5.com
0625

April Cross, USA
www.acrosscakes.shutterfly.com
acrosstx@att.net
0388

www.cupcakeavenue.co.uk, Baiju Patel & Alpa Patel, **Cupcake Avenue Limited**, UK
info@cupcakeavenue.co.uk
0191, 0410, 0577, 0695

Cupcakes Nouveau, Cristina Valdes & Shayrin Badillo, USA
www.cupcakesnouveau.com
info@cupcakesnouveau.com
0017, 0135, 0247, 0658, 0733

The Cupcake Tarts, Michelle Groenewald & Kim de Villiers, South Africa
www.flickr.com/photos/tuttabella
tuttabella@iafrica.com
0089, 0351, 0419, 0464, 0629, 0649, 0689, 0814

Colleen Davis, **Little Miss Cake**, USA
www.littlemisscake.com
me@littlemisscake.com
0069, 0266, 0296, 0315-0319, 0382, 0383, 0398, 0422, 0592, 0620, 0728, 0759, 0829, 0842

Marieke de Korte, **Alle Taarten**, The Netherlands
www.alletaarten.nl
info@alletaarten.nl
0001, 0473, 0487, 0866, 0912

Elif Alkac Dedeoglu, **Elif'in Kurabiyeleri**, Turkey
http://elifscookies.blogspot.com
www.elifinkurabiyeleri.com
elif.alkac@gmail.com
0030, 0129, 0474, 0476, 0569, 0887

Tammy Denmark, USA
www.southerncottagecakery.com
zoey2jack@yahoo.com
0173, 0342, 0404, 0515, 0561, 0742, 0775

Julaine Denny, USA
www.theresalwaysroomfordessert.blogspot.com
nj1124@comcast.net
0753

Nancy Didion, USA
nancy@nancydidion.com
0267, 0270, 0384, 0395, 0424, 0595, 0599, 0638, 0724, 0755, 0811, 0812, 0821, 0923

Melissa Diedtrich, USA
http://oohlalacakes.blogspot.com
melissa.diedtrich@gmail.com
0380, 0826, 0850

Sharnel Dollar, The Cupcake Company,
Australia
www.thecupcakecompany.com.au
grumeti76@mac.com
0149, 0188, 0278, 0289, 0509, 0527, 0880

Loren Ebert, www.thebakingsheet.blogspot.
com, USA
lorenoneill@aol.com
0466, 0734, 0736

Sumayya Eichmann, Mio Cupcakes, Australia
www.miocupcakes.blogspot.com
sumi.01@hotmail.com
0116, 0414, 0490, 0704, 0833, 0835

Donna Erskine, Australia
erskine83@live.com.au
0381, 0411, 0436, 0747

Elizabeth Evenz & Erin Salerno,
Elizabeth's Cakes, USA
www.elizabethscakes.com
esalerno78@yahoo.com
0078, 0900, 0947

Madeleine Farias, Madzcakes, Australia
www.flickr.com/photos/madzcakes
madzcakes@yahoo.com
0097, 0326, 0349, 0396, 0407, 0510, 0540,
0708, 0737, 0798

April Farnum, USA
0645, 0822

Kathy Finholt, Kathy's Kakes, LLC, USA
www.kathyskakesllc.com
kathyskakesllc@gmail.com
0136, 0251, 0862, 0868, 0915, 0925, 0926

www.fireandicing.com, Dante Ramon Nuño,
USA
dante@fireandicing.com
0076, 0187, 0300, 0442, 0469, 0514,
0628, 0693, 0764, 1000

Liis Florides, www.tourtes.com, Cyprus
mflorides@cytanet.com.cy; cakes@tourtes.com
0155, 0310-0314, 0367, 0517, 0521, 0525,
0560, 0601, 0790, 0896, 0955

Myriam Sánchez Garcia, Chapix Cookies,
Mexico
www.chapixcookies.com
contacto@chapixcookies.com
0415, 0430-0432, 0444, 0465, 0499-0505, 0671

Alexandra Gardner, USA
alexandrahgardner@gmail.com
0421

Klaire Garnica, The Little Cupcakery, Australia
www.thelittlecupcakery.com.au
klaire@thelittlecupcakery.com.au
0002, 0025, 0054, 0200, 0249, 0252, 0390, 0472,
0539, 0550, 0610, 0618, 0619, 0636, 0687, 0748

Morgan Garrison, USA
www.morganscakes.blogspot.com
morgangarrison123@yahoo.com
0571

Paula P. Gati, Cookie Queen LI, USA
www.cookiequeenli.blogspot.com/
cookiequeenli@aol.com
0160, 0207, 0519

Jeannie Gearin, www.cakesbyjeannie.com,
USA
jmgearin@juno.com
0498

Lorena Gil V., Cupcakes & More, Switzerland
www.moresweetcupcakes.blogspot.com
c_lorena24@hotmail.com
0021, 0082, 0121, 0127, 0130, 0151, 0236,
0258, 0273, 0344, 0399, 0612

Joshua Gomes, Veronica's Treats, USA
www.veronicastreats.com
krankychef1701@aol.com
0022

Jill Gosnell, Indy Cakes, USA
www.indycakes.com
info@indycakes.com
0285, 0387, 0681

Gumdrop Cookie Shop, USA
www.gumdropcookieshop.com
thea@gumdropcookieshop.com
0096, 0228, 0463, 0467, 0568, 0971

Peggy Hambright, MagPies Bakery, USA
www.magpiescakes.com
www.johnblackphotography.com
0137, 0203, 0260, 0262, 0452, 0489, 0512,
0588, 0669, 0696, 0727, 0901, 0957

Lisa Hansen, The Whole Cake and Caboodle,
New Zealand
darryn.and.lisa.hansen@xtra.co.nz
0016, 0119, 0126, 0157, 0163, 0213, 0231, 0255,
0354, 0394, 0614, 0630, 0746, 0800, 0803

Nayeli Hartman, Itty Bitty Cake Shop, USA
www.ittybittycakeshop.com
nayeli@ittybittycakeshop.com
0851

Susie Hazard, SusieHazCakes, USA
susie@callsusie.com
0150, 0324, 0441, 0493, 0537, 0547, 0564,
0807, 0935

Asa Hellgren, Hello Sugar!, Sweden
www.hellosugar.se
asa@hellosugar.se
0011, 0012, 0014, 0015, 0117, 0125, 0152,
0417, 0723, 0774

Marisa Hess, USA
www.flickr.com/josefs
marisahess@hotmail.com
0181, 0224, 0264, 0281, 0455, 0678, 0879,
0885, 0922, 0963, 0972, 0973, 0979

Tracy Lynn Hicks, USA
tracyhicksdesigns@yahoo.com
0470, 0557, 0589, 0590, 0591, 0593, 0600,
0606, 0776

Michelle Hollinshead, Cameo Cupcakes, UK
www.cameocupcakes.co.uk
michelle@cameocupcakes.co.uk
0217, 0552, 0652

Patricia Holmes, Fondant.com, USA
www.fondant.com
patricia@fondant.com
0475, 0496, 0549, 0555, 0570, 0965

Lynette Horner, Cakes by Lynette, UK
www.cakesbylynette.co.uk
cakesbylynette@yahoo.co.uk
0077, 0115, 0219, 0294, 0350, 0365, 0524, 0624,
0701

Carla Luisa Iglesias, www.ckdreams.net, USA
clsiglesias@yahoo.com; carla@ckdreams.net
0335-0338

Cassie Indari, Cakes by Cassie, Australia
cakesbycassie@optusnet.com.au
0386, 0522, 0782

Dina Isham, Designer Cakes by the LadyGloom, Malaysia
www.flickr.com/photos/theladygloom
theladygloom@gmail.com
0075, 0197, 0453, 0545, 0768, 0816, 0824, 0924

Vanessa Iti, Bella Cupcakes, New Zealand
www.bellacupcakes.blogspot.com
bellacupcakes@hotmail.com
0050, 0053, 0056, 0057, 0094, 0095, 0100,
0331, 0373, 0377, 0378, 0439, 0583, 0584,
0810, 0867, 0891

Noemi Jaime, Mexico
www.mimi-creation.blogspot.com
mimi_creations@hotmail.com
0087, 0297, 0372, 0686, 0705

Sharon Keller, Cake it up a Notch, USA
cakeitupanotch@live.com
0558, 0882, 0898

Monique Kleine, Cupcake Treats, Australia
http://www.cupcaketreats.com
monnie@cupcaketreats.com
0177, 0178, 0562

Dot Klerck, Cupcakes By Design, South Africa
www.cupcakesbydesign.co.za
dot@cupcakesbydesign.co.za
0048, 0074, 0113, 0122, 0141, 0202, 0254,
0302, 0403, 0483, 0634, 0688

Yen Le, www.le-cupcake.com, Canada
contact@le-cupcake.com
0006-0009, 0284

Samantha Lee, Haus of Cake, Australia
www.hausofcake.com.au
hausofcake@yahoo.com.au
0374, 0389, 0993

Mylene Lee, Lithia, FL, USA
leehomework@gmail.com;
cakesbymylene@gmail.com
0597

Alissa Levine, Pastry Girl Cakes, USA
www.pastrygirlcakes.com
info@pastrygirlcakes.com
0582, 0805

Amanda Linton, House of Sweets, USA
www.houseofsweetsbakery.com
amanda@houseofsweetsbakery.com
0020, 0259, 0287, 0292, 0323, 0328, 0357,
0531, 0668, 0721

The Little Cakery, Svarna Singh, UK
www.thelittlecakery.co.uk
eat@thelittlecakery.co.uk
0023, 0026, 0085, 0128, 0146, 0166, 0256,
0405, 0478, 0484, 0858

Rhienn Davis, Look Cupcake, USA
www.lookcupcake.com
www.lookcupcake.blogspot.com
order@lookcupcake.com
0261, 0516, 0603

June Lynch, Picture Perfect Cake, Canada
www.pictureperfectcakeart.com.
info@pictureperfectcakeart.com
0043, 0162, 0960, 0970, 0994

Monica Mancini, USA
mojo3799@optonline.net
0494

Dana Marcus, Cupcakes By Dana, USA
www.cupcakesbydana.com
cakeorder@cupcakesbydana.com
0643, 0754

Susana Martinez Zepeda, Casa Susana, Mexico
www.casasusana.com.mx
casasusana_mz@yahoo.com.mx
0107, 0283, 0362, 0804

Lisa Martins, Australia
moonstone@amnet.net.au
0186

Aileen Master, A Master Creation, USA
aileen@amastercreation.com
0438, 0572, 0615, 0661, 0679, 0718, 0749, 0771

Farnaz RouzParast Menhaji, USA
www.eleganttreats.vpweb.com
frouzparast1@yahoo.com
0073, 0921

Gina Milton, Just Desserts, USA
www.justdessertsfl.webs.com
justdessertsfl@yahoo.com
0967

Robyn Morrison, Canada
rdmorrison@cogeco.ca
0047, 0218, 0836, 0998

Meaghan Mountford, Chic Cookies, USA
www.chiccookiekits.com;
www.chiccookiekits.blogspot.com
chiccookiekits@yahoo.com
0334, 0340, 0445-0449, 0480, 0596, 0635,
0662, 0740, 0794, 0795

Yuhalini Narendran, Party With Cakes, Malaysia
www.partywithcakes.com
yuha@partywithcakes.com;
yuhalini@yahoo.com
0968

Jene Nato a/k/a Rylan Ty, USA
www.artandappetite.com
artandapptite@yahoo.com
0888, 0890

Shelly Netherton, Country Kitchen SweetArt, USA
www.countrykitchensa.com
catalog@countrykitchensa.com
0059, 0479, 0729, 0779, 0786

Emma O'Shaughnessy, Baker's Treat, UK
www.bakerstreat.co.uk
emma@bakerstreat.co.uk
0068, 0088, 0140, 0391, 0641, 0939

Cindy J. Patrick, Enticing Icings and Custom Cakes, USA
www.enticingicings.com
enticingicings@columbus.rr.com
0943

Belinda Patton, www.belisacupcakes.com.au, Australia
belisacupcakes@yahoo.com.au
0042, 0147, 0167, 0198, 0208, 0226, 0426, 0529,
0832, 0886, 0893

Layla Pegado Couto, Layla Pegado Cakes, UK
www.laylacakes.com;
www.laylapegadocakes.blogspot.com
laylapegado@hotmail.com
0019, 0159, 0171, 0401, 0818

Peggy's Cupcakes, Rosalind Miller, UK
www.peggyscupcakes.co.uk
info@peggyscupcakes.co.uk
0164, 0245, 0739, 0788, 0905, 0988

Fiona Perham, sugarsugar, UK
www.sugarsugarcreations.com
fiona.perham@sugarsugarcreations.com
0045, 0123, 0144, 0673, 0674

Piamarianne, Kageriet.net, Pia Kristensen,
Denmark
www.kageriet.net
piamarianne@kageriet.net
0104, 0138, 0176, 0450, 0650, 0702, 0719,
0785, 0881, 0902

Shellane Pickett, Apple-Butter Bakery and
Custom Cake Shoppe, USA
www.abccakeshoppe.com
shellane@abccakeshoppe.com
0106, 0108, 0838

Marian Poirier, Sweetopia, Canada
http://www.sweetopia.net
sweetopia@inbox.com
0551, 0598, 0611, 0621, 0763, 0799, 0849

Samantha Potter, USA
sweeteatscakes@comcast.net
0566, 0626

Sabrina Price, Renae Bradley, USA
sabrina_l_price@yahoo.com
0508

Valerie L. Quirarte, USA
www.flickr.com/photos/toodlesjupiter/
toodlesjupiter@prodigy.net
0170, 0528, 0546, 0770

Michelle Rea, Inspired by Michelle Cake
Designs, Australia
www.inspiredbymichelle.com.au
inspiredbymichelle@gmail.com
0065, 0329, 0345, 0370, 0408, 0507, 0797, 0877,
0996

Jeanine Reed, Cake Muffin, USA
www.facebook.com/cakemuffins
cakemuffingirl@yahoo.com
0743

Rick Reichart, cakelava, USA
www.cakelava.com
cakelava@hawaii.rr.com
0032-0037, 0594, 0738, 0865, 0876, 0934,
0941, 0958

Rene Takes the Cake, Rene Kauder, USA
www.renekauder.blogspot.com
kauderra@gmail.com
0192

Didem Resne, Turkey
www.didemscafe.blogspot.com; www.caferoyal-
kardelen.blogspot.com
caferoyals@gmail.com
0118, 0239, 0277, 0279, 0280, 0523, 0553,
0556, 0613, 0730, 0953, 0992

Amanda Rettke, USA
http://iammommy.typepad.com/i_am_baker/
manda2177@aol.com
0248, 0477, 0492, 0660, 0667, 0685

Marie Richter, Maries Hobby Corner, Sweden
www.marieshobbycorner.se
maries.hobbycorner@bredband.net
0242, 0286, 0356, 0412, 0544

Sylvia Rivas, Tough Cookie Bakery, USA
flickr.com/photos/chocolatemoosecakes
chocmocakes@yahoo.com
0052, 0246, 0307, 0416, 0623, 0758, 0878, 0989

Jackie Rodriguez, www.lasdeliciasdevivir.com,
Dominican Republic
0193, 0205, 0481, 0488, 0605

Maryann Rollins, The Cookie Artisan, USA
0216, 0332, 0385, 0392, 0454, 0497, 0548, 0574,
0617, 0631, 0632, 0716, 0725, 0726

Rose Petals Cakery, RoseMarie Carvallo, USA
www.rosepetalscakery.com
rose@rosepetalscakery.com
0055, 0081, 0134, 0533, 0752, 0801, 0991

www.roseysugar.com, Japan
info@roseysugar.com
0222, 0223, 0233, 0305, 0780

Erin Salerno, USA
www.flickr.com/photos/cakesbyerinsalerno
esalerno78@yahoo.com
0325, 0848, 0980

Emily Schildhouse, USA
emily.schildhouse@gmail.com
0677

Dimitrana Schinogl, Austria
www.dimitranas.blogspot.com
dimitrana_s@yahoo.com
0027, 0086, 0101, 0111, 0183, 0220, 0460, 0581,
0651

Debbie Schwartz, Debbie's Cakes, Israel
www.flickr.com/photos/debbiescakes
debbiecakes123@gmail.com
0013, 0227, 0240, 0717, 0919

Scrumptious Buns, Samantha Douglass, UK
www.scrumptiousbuns.co.uk
sam@scrumptiousbuns.co.uk
0275, 0346, 0530, 0744, 0751, 0784, 0840, 0977

Liz Shim, EatCakeBeMerry, USA
www.eatcakebemerry.com
eatcakebemerry@gmail.com
0031, 0209, 0787, 0864, 0913, 0964, 0986

Helen Shipman, Boudoir Cakes, UK
www.boudoircakes.com
boudoircakes@hotmail.com
0029, 0058, 0190, 0952, 0969

Cecille L. Sia, Tongued-Tied With Sweetest
Delight Cakes & Pastry, Philippines
wwwcecillesia.multiphy.com/88db.ph-
weddingcakes/cakes
clsia70@yahoo.com
0871, 0981

Dolores Silfven & Karen Silfven, USA
0486

Annette Simpson, Canada
www.sunflowerscreations.ca
asimpson2@telus.net
0214, 0221

Lindy Smith, Lindy's Cakes Ltd, UK
www.lindyscakes.co.uk
0265, 0440, 0482, 0722, 0756, 0861, 0869,
0918, 0930, 0944-0946, 0950, 0984

Leslie Srodek-Johnson, Stan's Northfield
Bakery, USA
www.stansbakery.com
leslie@stansbakery.com
0051, 0139

Amy Stella, www.cakesuniquesbyamy.com, USA
amystella@comcast.net
0291, 0293, 0320, 0322, 0327, 0358, 0359, 0397, 0672, 0817, 0834, 0932, 0948, 0987

Alison Sturge, Alison Wonderland Cakes, USA
www.alisonwonderlandcakes.com
townlakecakes@gmail.com
0640, 0920

www.sugar-couture.com, Penny Stankiewicz, Sugar Couture LLC, USA
penny@sugar-couture.com
0253, 0271, 0298, 0309, 0608, 0637, 0654, 0735, 0745, 0857

Tang Meng Choo, Mongstirs, Singapore
www.mongstirs.com
kymclim@gmail.com
0185, 0585, 0646

Amy Teoh Say See, Mom & Daughter Cakes, Malaysia
www.mndcakes.com; www.blog.mndcakes.com
mndcakes@gmail.com
0348, 0406, 0710, 0827, 0841

Sheryl Thai, Cupcake Central, Australia
www.cupcakecentral.com.au
info@cupcakecentral.com.au
0195, 0376, 0769, 0852

Bridget Thibeault, Flour Girl, USA
www.flourgirl.net
brigget@flourgirl.net
0040, 0102, 0212, 0793, 0831, 0978, 0985

Shinni Tock, www.bakincow.com, Singapore
bakincow@yahoo.com.sg
0586

Diane Trap, USA
dtrapbakes@gmail.com
0091, 0666

Susan E. Turnbull, Anyone for Cake?, UK
www.anyoneforcakescotland.co.uk
enquiries@anyoneforcakescotland.co.uk
0143, 0765

Vanilla Bake Shop, Santa Monica, Amy Berman, USA
www.vanillabakeshop.com
sweets@vanillabakeshop.com;
amy@vanillabakeshop.com
0067, 0132, 0928

Nicole Varganyi, Krazy Kakes, Canada
www.nicskrazykakes.com
krazyk@rogers.com
0962

Alena Vaughn, Alena's Sweets, USA
www.alenassweets.blogspot.com
alenavaughn@gmailcom
0206, 0303, 0933, 0954, 0982, 0983

Annette Villaverde, Ladybug Luggage Gourmet Cookies & Cakes LLC, USA
www.ladybugluggage.com
ladybugluggage@gmail.com
0060, 0062, 0064, 0145, 0554, 0575, 0587, 0633, 0683

Susy Wangsawidjaja, Kuki Cupcakes, Indonesia
www.kukicupcakes.com
swangsawidjaja@bankbii.com;
info@kukicupcakes.com
0038, 0230, 0676, 0703, 0707, 0777, 0825

Anna Wawzonek, Anna Elizabeth Cakes, Canada
www.annaelizabethcakes.com
annaelizabethcakes@hotmail.com
0418, 0974, 0990

Catherine Webb, www.cathysdesignercookies.com, USA
cathy@cathysdesignercookies.com
0443, 0579, 0580, 0761

Dahlia Weinman, Dahlia's Custom Cakes, USA
www.dahliascakes.com
dahlia@dahliascakes.com
0079, 0148, 0204, 0250, 0457, 0462, 0535, 0809, 0959, 0995

Linda Nielsen Wermeling, Holy Sweet, Sweden
www.holysweet.blogspot.com; www.holysweet.se
linda@holysweet.se
0070, 0196, 0409, 0856, 0859, 0874, 0906, 0966

Jennifer Whitlock, Posh Pastries, USA
www.posh-pastries.com
jen.whitlock@gmail.com
0371, 0647, 0664, 0670, 0762

Monica Williams, Delissimon, New Zealand
www.delissimon.blogspot.com
delissimon@vodafone.co.nz
0845, 0846

Jennifer Wolak, USA
www.blempgorf.blogspot.com
blempgorf@gmail.com
0731, 0766

Johanna Wulff, Johanna Wulff—Cakes & Cookies, USA
www.johannawulff.blogspot.com
jwulffdebriz@yahoo.com
0375

Jen Yap, A Little Slice of Heaven, Australia
www.alsoheaven.com.au
jen.yap@alsoheaven.com.au
0156, 0189, 0194, 0339, 0341, 0433, 0773, 0872, 0875, 0892, 0942

acknowledgments

Thanks to the gang at Quarry for once again allowing us to indulge in a fantasy game of collecting the tastiest ideas and images from all over the world! Mary Ann, you were (as always) our bright guiding light through a sea of fondant. Cora and Betsy, your organizational skills and positive attitudes made the process sweet all the way through. David—you're always there when we need you! Winnie and Rosalind, your clear editorial and art direction defines the quality of Quarry's books, time and time again.

The bakers included here are to whom this book is dedicated. Not only are their talents sublime, but through collaboration via online communities such as Flickr groups, their photography skills are becoming top notch (as you can see in this book)! The groups are supportive and encouraging, and are conscientious in giving their peers credit for original ideas. If you're a home baker or independent bakery like our contributors, we highly recommend that you join a Flickr pool or two to meet these artisans yourself.

The wonderful icing recipes were graciously contributed by Kate Sullivan, author of *Kate's Cake Decorating* and founder of LovinSullivanCakes (www.cakepower.com). Thanks, Kate!

From Sandra: Gina, simply: I couldn't have done it without you! In fact, I **wouldn't** have done it without you.

From Gina: A big thank you goes to my sister, Sandra Salamony, who knows how to make everything (and everyone) look good. What better talent is there? And, the biggest thanks goes to my husband, Scott (a/k/a "Mr. Pie"), for his constant good humor, and I don't mean ice cream!

From us both: Thanks to our father, Gene Salamony, for instilling the importance of art from an early age. Also for making the best lemon meringue pie in Michigan!

And to our mother, Karen Silfven, thank you for making sure we lived with beauty (and German's Chocolate Cake) every day.

about the authors

Artist, designer, and author **Sandra Salamony** lives by the beautiful shores of Lake Michigan with her mini schnauzer, Officer Mike, and feline valet, Monty. Her previous Quarry 1000 books include *1000 Artisan Textiles* (also with Gina M. Brown), and *1000 Jewelry Inspirations*. She is an award-winning encaustic artist and graphic designer, and in her free time she plays banjo with The Amazing Cherry Pickers. You can see more of her work at SandraSalamony.com.

Gina M. Brown is an architect, amateur baker, and textile artist. She lives with her husband, Scott (who doubles as a taste-tester), their golden retriever, Zinger, and two frisky cats in Michigan, a source of infinite agricultural, horticultural, and overall cultural inspiration. Her work has appeared in *Hand Lettering for Crafts* and various University of Michigan publications. She previously collaborated with her sister on *1000 Artisan Textiles*, also for Quarry Books.